OSINT HACKER'S ARSENAL

METAGOOFIL, THEHARVESTER, MITAKA, BUILTWITH

4 BOOKS IN 1

BOOK 1
OSINT HACKER'S ARSENAL: UNVEILING THE ESSENTIALS

BOOK 2
MASTERING OSINT: ADVANCED TECHNIQUES WITH MITAKA

BOOK 3
EXPERT OSINT STRATEGIES: HARNESSING BUILTWITH FOR PROFOUND INSIGHTS

BOOK 4
THE ULTIMATE OSINT HANDBOOK: FROM NOVICE TO PRO WITH COMPREHENSIVE TOOLKITS

ROB BOTWRIGHT

Published by Rob Botwright
Library of Congress Cataloging-in-Publication Data
ISBN 978-1-83938-635-0
Cover design by Rizzo

Disclaimer

The contents of this book are based on extensive research and the best available historical sources. However, the author and publisher make no claims, promises, or guarantees about the accuracy, completeness, or adequacy of the information contained herein. The information in this book is provided on an "as is" basis, and the author and publisher disclaim any and all liability for any errors, omissions, or inaccuracies in the information or for any actions taken in reliance on such information. The opinions and views expressed in this book are those of the author and do not necessarily reflect the official policy or position of any organization or individual mentioned in this book. Any reference to specific people, places, or events is intended only to provide historical context and is not intended to defame or malign any group, individual, or entity. The information in this book is intended for educational and entertainment purposes only. It is not intended to be a substitute for professional advice or judgment. Readers are encouraged to conduct their own research and to seek professional advice where appropriate. Every effort has been made to obtain necessary permissions and acknowledgments for all images and other copyrighted material used in this book. Any errors or omissions in this regard are unintentional, and the author and publisher will correct them in future editions.

BOOK 1 - OSINT HACKER'S ARSENAL: UNVEILING THE ESSENTIALS

Introduction 5
Chapter 1: Introduction to OSINT 8
Chapter 2: Setting Up Your OSINT Environment 14
Chapter 3: Metagoofil: Harvesting Metadata 22
Chapter 4: theHarvester: Gathering Email Intelligence 28
Chapter 5: Mitaka: Automating OSINT Tasks 35
Chapter 6: BuiltWith: Profiling Website Technologies 42
Chapter 7: Social Media Investigations 50
Chapter 8: Geolocation and Mapping 57
Chapter 9: Advanced Search Techniques 65
Chapter 10: Legal and Ethical Considerations in OSINT 73

BOOK 2 - MASTERING OSINT: ADVANCED TECHNIQUES WITH MITAKA

Chapter 1: Exploring the Power of Mitaka 81
Chapter 2: Customizing Mitaka for Your OSINT Needs 88
Chapter 3: Leveraging Automation for OSINT Success 95
Chapter 4: Targeted Data Collection with Mitaka 103
Chapter 5: Mitaka and Social Media Intelligence 110
Chapter 6: Advanced Analysis and Visualization 117
Chapter 7: Cross-Platform Integration with Mitaka 126
Chapter 8: Mitaka in Red Team Operations 134
Chapter 9: Mitaka for Threat Intelligence 142
Chapter 10: Mitaka Best Practices and Case Studies 150

BOOK 3 - EXPERT OSINT STRATEGIES: HARNESSING BUILTWITH FOR PROFOUND INSIGHTS

Chapter 1: The Power of BuiltWith in OSINT 158
Chapter 2: Advanced Techniques for BuiltWith Profiling 165
Chapter 3: Extracting Hidden Gems with BuiltWith 172
Chapter 4: BuiltWith and E-commerce Intelligence 181
Chapter 5: BuiltWith for Competitive Analysis 190
Chapter 6: BuiltWith and Cybersecurity Investigations 197
Chapter 7: Deep Dive into Technology Stacks 205
Chapter 8: Building Custom OSINT Pipelines with BuiltWith 212
Chapter 9: BuiltWith in Corporate Investigations 218
Chapter 10: Case Studies in Expert OSINT with BuiltWith 225

BOOK 4 - THE ULTIMATE OSINT HANDBOOK: FROM NOVICE TO PRO WITH COMPREHENSIVE TOOLKITS

Chapter 1: Introduction to Open Source Intelligence 232
Chapter 2: Building Your OSINT Toolkit 235
Chapter 3: Essential OSINT Techniques for Novices 243
Chapter 4: Leveraging Advanced OSINT Tools 251
Chapter 5: Metagoofil Unleashed: A Deep Dive 259
Chapter 6: theHarvester's Secrets: Advanced Email Discovery 267
Chapter 7: Mastering Mitaka: Automation and Integration 274
Chapter 8: In-Depth Profiling with BuiltWith 280
Chapter 9: Specialized OSINT Approaches 287
Chapter 10: Real-world OSINT Applications and Case Studies 293
Conclusion 299

Introduction

Welcome to the "OSINT Hacker's Arsenal" book bundle, an immersive journey into the dynamic realm of Open Source Intelligence (OSINT). This collection of four distinct volumes, each centered around powerful OSINT tools, is designed to equip you with the knowledge and skills to navigate the complex landscape of online information gathering and analysis.

In an age where data is abundant and readily accessible, the ability to harness this wealth of information is invaluable. OSINT, with its vast array of techniques and tools, empowers individuals and organizations to uncover hidden insights, solve complex problems, and make informed decisions.

Our journey begins with "Book 1 - OSINT Hacker's Arsenal: Unveiling the Essentials," where we delve into the fundamental concepts and core tools that underpin the world of OSINT. Metagoofil, theHarvester, Mitaka, and BuiltWith are your companions as you embark on your OSINT adventure, uncovering the potential of these essential tools.

"Book 2 - Mastering OSINT: Advanced Techniques with Mitaka" propels you into the realm of advanced OSINT strategies. Mitaka, a powerful automation and integration platform, becomes your key to streamlining OSINT tasks and conducting thorough investigations. By exploring customization, integration, and best practices, you'll elevate your OSINT skills to new heights.

In "Book 3 - Expert OSINT Strategies: Harnessing BuiltWith for Profound Insights," you'll harness the capabilities of BuiltWith, a versatile tool for profiling website technologies. Uncover hidden details within technology stacks, master competitive analysis, and apply BuiltWith to corporate investigations. This volume equips you with the expertise to make data-driven decisions and gain a competitive edge.

Our journey culminates in "Book 4 - The Ultimate OSINT Handbook: From Novice to Pro with Comprehensive Toolkits." Here, we guide you from novice to professional, arming you with comprehensive toolkits and deep insights into OSINT ethics and legal considerations. Real-world case studies illustrate the practical application of your newfound knowledge.

Throughout this book bundle, our goal is not only to empower you with technical skills but also to instill a sense of responsibility and ethics in your OSINT practices. As you embark on this educational voyage, remember that the knowledge you gain carries a significant responsibility to use it wisely, ethically, and responsibly.

Prepare to unlock the potential of OSINT, from its essentials to advanced strategies, as you explore the diverse tools and techniques at your disposal. Whether you're a beginner seeking a solid foundation or an experienced practitioner looking to expand your expertise, the "OSINT Hacker's Arsenal" book bundle is your comprehensive guide to success in the world of Open Source Intelligence. Welcome to the journey.

BOOK 1
OSINT HACKER'S ARSENAL
UNVEILING THE ESSENTIALS

ROB BOTWRIGHT

Chapter 1: Introduction to OSINT

OSINT, or Open Source Intelligence, forms the bedrock of modern-day investigative and research efforts. It is an approach to gathering and analyzing information from publicly available sources to obtain valuable insights. Understanding the foundations of OSINT is crucial for anyone seeking to harness its power effectively. At its core, OSINT relies on the principle that a wealth of information exists in the open domain, waiting to be discovered and utilized. This information can come from a wide range of sources, including the internet, social media, public records, and more.

The advent of the internet has significantly transformed the landscape of information gathering. With the proliferation of online platforms, data is being generated and shared at an unprecedented rate. Consequently, the field of OSINT has evolved to keep pace with these changes. To embark on an OSINT journey, one must first grasp the key principles that underpin this discipline. These principles are founded on legality, ethics, and methodology.

Ethical considerations are paramount when conducting OSINT. It is imperative to respect individuals' privacy and adhere to applicable laws and regulations. Conducting OSINT ethically ensures that the information obtained is both reliable and actionable. A core tenet of OSINT is to gather information from sources that are publicly accessible. This implies that the information one collects should not involve hacking, intrusion, or any unauthorized access to private systems or data.

Legal boundaries must be navigated with care. Different countries have their own laws and regulations regarding data privacy and information gathering. It is essential to be aware of and compliant with these laws to avoid legal consequences. Beyond ethical and legal considerations, OSINT methodology plays a crucial role in the quality and effectiveness of the gathered intelligence.

An effective OSINT process typically involves several key steps. The first step is defining the objectives and goals of the investigation or research. What specific information is needed, and what is the purpose of obtaining it? Once the objectives are clear, it is time to plan the OSINT strategy. This includes identifying the sources that are likely to contain the required information and outlining the methods and tools to be used.

The execution phase involves actively collecting information from the identified sources. This can involve searching online databases, monitoring social media, scraping websites, and more. During this phase, it is essential to ensure data accuracy and relevance. Information collected should be verified through multiple sources whenever possible to minimize the risk of misinformation or bias.

Analysis is a critical aspect of OSINT, where the collected information is examined, and patterns, trends, or insights are identified. This is where the true value of OSINT often emerges, as it can provide unique perspectives and actionable intelligence. Effective analysis may require specialized skills and tools, such as data visualization or link analysis software.

Communication of findings is the final step in the OSINT process. The insights gained should be conveyed clearly and concisely to the intended audience. Whether it's a report for a client, a presentation for colleagues, or information for personal use, the delivery of OSINT results should align with the objectives set at the outset.

In addition to these core principles and steps, OSINT practitioners often rely on a wide range of tools and techniques to enhance their effectiveness. These tools can include search engines, social media monitoring platforms, web scraping software, and more. The choice of tools depends on the specific requirements of the OSINT operation and the available resources.

It is worth noting that OSINT is not limited to any particular domain or industry. It is a versatile discipline with applications in fields such as cybersecurity, competitive intelligence, law enforcement, journalism, corporate investigations, and more. The versatility of OSINT lies in its ability to adapt to diverse objectives and contexts.

Moreover, OSINT is not static; it continues to evolve alongside technological advancements and changes in information sharing. New sources of information emerge, and the methods for accessing and analyzing data constantly develop. Therefore, staying updated with the latest trends and technologies in OSINT is essential for practitioners.

In summary, OSINT is a powerful and ethical approach to gathering intelligence from publicly available sources. Its foundations rest on legality, ethics, and methodology. OSINT practitioners must navigate the ethical and legal landscape while employing a systematic approach to gather, analyze, and communicate intelligence effectively. With the right principles, methods, and tools, OSINT can provide valuable insights and contribute to informed decision-making in various fields and industries.

To understand the historical context of OSINT, we must delve into the origins of intelligence gathering. Throughout human history, information has been a valuable asset in decision-making and conflict resolution. In ancient times, leaders relied on spies, scouts, and informants to collect intelligence about their adversaries. These early forms of intelligence gathering laid the groundwork for the modern concept of OSINT.

The evolution of OSINT can be traced back to the 19th and early 20th centuries when intelligence agencies and military organizations recognized the need for systematic data collection from open sources. During World War I, the significance of analyzing publicly available information became evident, as both Allied and Central Powers sought to gain an edge through intelligence. Newspapers, publications, and public records served as sources of valuable information.

The term "Open Source Intelligence" was officially coined in the 1980s within the U.S. military. It referred to the systematic collection and analysis of publicly available information to support military and national security efforts. During the Cold War, OSINT gained prominence as a means to gather intelligence on the activities and intentions of rival nations.

The end of the Cold War marked a shift in the focus of OSINT. With the rise of the internet and the proliferation of digital information, the scope of OSINT expanded significantly. OSINT practitioners now had access to a vast amount of online data, including websites, forums, social media, and databases.

The 21st century saw OSINT becoming increasingly relevant in various domains, including counterterrorism, cybersecurity, law enforcement, corporate investigations, and competitive intelligence. The September 11, 2001 attacks in the United States highlighted the importance of open source intelligence in preventing and responding to threats.

The internet played a pivotal role in the transformation of OSINT. Online forums, blogs, and social media platforms became valuable sources of information for OSINT analysts. Tools and techniques for web scraping, data mining, and social media monitoring emerged to facilitate the collection and analysis of online data.

The concept of "Big Data" further propelled OSINT into the forefront of intelligence gathering. The ability to process and analyze massive volumes of data from open sources became a critical asset in decision-making. This led to the development of advanced data analytics and visualization tools tailored for OSINT purposes.

The open source nature of OSINT also led to its democratization. While governments and intelligence agencies have historically been the primary users of intelligence, OSINT empowered individuals, researchers, journalists, and private sector entities to harness its capabilities. This democratization enabled a broader range of applications for OSINT.

The role of OSINT in the digital age extends beyond traditional intelligence operations. It plays a crucial role in cybersecurity, helping organizations identify vulnerabilities and threats by monitoring online chatter and data breaches. It is also instrumental in reputation management, where businesses and individuals use OSINT to monitor their online presence and assess their public image.

The use of OSINT in law enforcement has expanded to include investigations into cybercrimes, fraud, and online threats. It assists in locating missing persons, tracking criminal activities, and identifying potential threats to public safety. OSINT techniques have become essential tools for modern policing.

In the corporate world, OSINT is used for competitive intelligence, market research, due diligence, and risk assessment. Companies analyze publicly available data to gain insights into their competitors, market trends, and potential business opportunities. This information informs strategic decisions and helps organizations stay competitive.

Journalists and media organizations rely on OSINT to verify information, fact-check stories, and uncover hidden details. Investigative journalists use OSINT to uncover corruption, expose wrongdoing, and provide accurate reporting to the public.

The historical context of OSINT underscores its adaptability and relevance in an ever-changing information landscape. From its origins in espionage and military intelligence to its current applications in diverse fields, OSINT continues to evolve as a vital tool for decision-makers, researchers, and analysts. In an era defined by information abundance, the principles and practices of OSINT remain at the forefront of information gathering and analysis.

Chapter 2: Setting Up Your OSINT Environment

To embark on your journey into the world of OSINT, it is essential to begin with the basics, and that starts with the installation of the necessary tools and software. These tools are the building blocks of your OSINT toolkit, enabling you to collect, analyze, and manage the wealth of information available in the open domain. Before delving into the specifics of each tool, it's crucial to understand the importance of a structured approach to their installation.

A well-organized OSINT toolkit ensures efficiency and ease of use throughout your investigations and research endeavors. The first step in this process is to assess your requirements and objectives. Depending on your needs, you may opt for a broad range of tools, each serving a specific purpose in the OSINT workflow. These tools can be categorized into various categories, including web scraping, data analysis, social media monitoring, and more.

Once you have a clear understanding of your goals, it's time to identify the tools that align with those objectives. Open source tools are often preferred in OSINT due to their accessibility and flexibility. However, there are also commercial tools available that offer advanced features and support. Your selection of tools should cater to your proficiency level, resources, and the nature of the OSINT operation.

Web scraping tools are fundamental in OSINT, as they allow you to extract data from websites and online platforms. Common web scraping tools include BeautifulSoup, Scrapy, and Selenium. BeautifulSoup, for instance, is a Python library that simplifies the parsing of HTML and XML documents, making it an excellent choice for web scraping tasks.

Data analysis tools are essential for making sense of the information you collect. These tools assist in processing, organizing, and visualizing data. Python libraries like Pandas and Matplotlib are popular choices for data manipulation and visualization. Pandas provides versatile data structures and functions for data analysis, while Matplotlib offers extensive capabilities for creating charts and graphs.

Social media monitoring tools enable you to track and analyze conversations, trends, and user activity on various social media platforms. Tools like Hootsuite and TweetDeck offer centralized dashboards for managing multiple social media accounts and monitoring mentions and hashtags. Additionally, specialized tools like Brandwatch and Talkwalker provide advanced sentiment analysis and social listening capabilities.

Web archiving tools are invaluable for preserving online content and capturing webpages for future reference. The Internet Archive's Wayback Machine is a widely known tool for archiving websites, allowing you to access historical versions of webpages. Other tools, such as Archive.is, also serve this purpose by capturing snapshots of web content.

Domain research tools assist in gathering information about domain names, websites, and their associated details. WHOIS databases and domain lookup services like WHOIS.net and ICANN Lookup provide insights into domain ownership, registration dates, and contact information. These tools are particularly useful for OSINT investigations involving websites and domains.

Network analysis tools aid in visualizing and understanding connections between entities, such as individuals, organizations, and websites. Gephi and Cytoscape are popular network analysis platforms that enable you to create interactive graphs and explore relationships within your OSINT data. These tools are especially valuable when investigating complex networks of information.

Geolocation tools play a crucial role in OSINT, allowing you to determine the physical locations of IP addresses, websites, or social media posts. GeoIP databases and services like MaxMind and IPinfo offer geolocation data, enabling you to map and analyze the geographical distribution of online entities. Geospatial information can be vital in investigations involving physical-world connections.

Investigative databases and search engines provide access to a vast array of public records, documents, and databases. Platforms like publicrecordsnow.com, Pipl, and Spokeo allow you to search for individuals, phone numbers, addresses, and more. These tools are instrumental in uncovering personal information and verifying identities during OSINT investigations.

Once you have identified the tools that align with your OSINT objectives, it's time to proceed with their installation. The installation process can vary depending on the tool and the operating system you are using. In most cases, open source tools can be installed using package managers or by downloading the software directly from their official websites.

For Python-based tools and libraries, the Python Package Index (PyPI) is a valuable resource for installation. You can use the pip package manager to install Python packages effortlessly. For example, to install BeautifulSoup, you can use the command "pip install beautifulsoup4." Similarly, Pandas and Matplotlib can be installed using "pip install pandas" and "pip install matplotlib," respectively.

Web scraping frameworks like Scrapy can also be installed using pip. Simply run the command "pip install scrapy" to set up Scrapy on your system. If you plan to use Selenium for web scraping, you can install it using "pip install selenium."

Social media monitoring tools often come with their own installation procedures, typically involving the download and installation of their respective desktop or web-based applications. These tools may also require account setup and configuration to connect to your social media accounts.

Web archiving tools like Archive.is and the Wayback Machine do not require installation, as they operate through web interfaces. Simply access their websites, enter the URL of the webpage you want to archive, and follow the provided instructions to capture and save the content.

Domain research tools may have different installation methods depending on the service or software. Some domain lookup services are web-based and do not require installation, while WHOIS databases may offer downloadable command-line tools for querying domain information.

Network analysis platforms like Gephi and Cytoscape are typically installed like traditional software applications. You can download the installation packages for your operating system from their official websites and follow the installation instructions provided.

Geolocation tools often come in the form of libraries or APIs that can be integrated into your OSINT projects. To use these tools, you may need to sign up for an API key or access credentials, which are usually provided by the service providers. Once you have the necessary credentials, you can incorporate geolocation capabilities into your OSINT scripts and applications.

Investigative databases and search engines are web-based platforms that require no installation. Access to these tools is typically subscription-based or may involve per-query fees. You can simply visit their websites and use their search and lookup functionalities as needed.

In summary, the installation of OSINT tools and software is a crucial step in preparing your OSINT toolkit for efficient and effective information gathering and analysis. By understanding your objectives, selecting the appropriate tools, and following installation procedures, you can ensure that your OSINT endeavors are well-equipped to meet your goals. With the right tools at your disposal, you can navigate the vast landscape of open source information with confidence and precision. Configuring the OSINT workspace is a critical step in preparing for your open-source intelligence (OSINT) activities. It involves setting up your environment, tools, and resources to ensure a smooth and efficient workflow. An organized and well-configured workspace is essential for collecting, analyzing, and managing the vast amount of information you will encounter during your OSINT investigations.

To begin the process of configuring your OSINT workspace, it's crucial to choose a dedicated and secure environment for your activities. Ideally, this environment should be isolated from your personal or work-related data to minimize the risk of accidental data leakage or security breaches. Consider using a separate computer or virtual machine for your OSINT work to maintain a clear boundary between your OSINT activities and other digital assets.

Selecting a secure and private network connection is equally important. OSINT often involves accessing public sources of information on the internet, but it's crucial to safeguard your own digital footprint. Using a virtual private network (VPN) or anonymizing tools like Tor can help protect your online identity and location. These precautions are especially relevant when conducting sensitive or confidential OSINT investigations.

When configuring your OSINT workspace, you'll need to choose an operating system that aligns with your objectives and tool preferences. While many OSINT tools are platform-agnostic and work on various operating systems, selecting the right OS can optimize your workflow. Linux distributions like Kali Linux and Parrot Security OS are popular choices among OSINT practitioners due to their pre-installed OSINT and security tools. However, you can configure your workspace on Windows or macOS as well, depending on your familiarity and requirements.

A critical aspect of OSINT configuration is the installation of essential software and tools. As mentioned earlier, your choice of tools will depend on your specific OSINT objectives, but there are some fundamental software components that every OSINT practitioner should consider. Web browsers like Mozilla Firefox and Google Chrome are essential for accessing online sources, and browser extensions like OSINT Framework can enhance your browsing experience by providing quick access to OSINT resources.

Text editors and note-taking applications are indispensable for organizing and documenting your findings. Popular text editors include Notepad++, Visual Studio Code, and Sublime Text, while note-taking tools like Evernote, OneNote, or even a simple text file can help you keep track of your research notes, URLs, and observations.

As you configure your workspace, consider using version control systems like Git to manage your OSINT projects and scripts. This allows you to track changes, collaborate with others, and maintain a history of your work. Additionally, setting up a reliable backup system is crucial to protect your data and ensure that you don't lose valuable information during your OSINT activities.

In the realm of virtualization, tools like VirtualBox or VMware can be invaluable for creating isolated virtual environments. These virtual machines can be used for testing potentially harmful scripts or tools without risking your primary OSINT workspace's integrity. This separation of environments enhances security and allows you to experiment safely.

When configuring your OSINT workspace, don't overlook the importance of maintaining a clean and organized file structure. Create well-defined directories or folders to categorize your OSINT projects, data, and scripts. This structure makes it easier to locate specific information and maintain an efficient workflow.

In addition to organizing your files, consider implementing naming conventions and labeling systems to help you quickly identify the content and context of your data. These practices ensure that your findings are easily accessible and comprehensible, especially when collaborating with others or revisiting previous investigations.

Security and privacy should always be at the forefront of your workspace configuration. Use strong, unique passwords for your accounts, and consider employing password management tools like LastPass or 1Password to securely store and manage your credentials. Encrypt sensitive data, both at rest and in transit, to protect it from unauthorized access. Implement firewalls and regularly update your operating system and software to patch security vulnerabilities.

Another crucial aspect of workspace configuration is the development of standardized workflows and procedures. Define clear and documented processes for your OSINT activities, from initial data collection to analysis and reporting. These standardized workflows not only enhance efficiency but also ensure consistency and repeatability in your investigations.

Furthermore, consider implementing a version control system for your OSINT projects and scripts. Version control allows you to track changes, collaborate with others, and maintain a history of your work. Popular version control platforms like Git and services like GitHub or GitLab provide robust tools for managing and sharing your OSINT code and research.

As part of your workspace configuration, establish a routine for data management and retention. Determine how long you should retain collected data, taking into account legal and ethical considerations. Develop a data disposal strategy to securely delete information that is no longer needed, and document your data retention policies to maintain compliance with privacy regulations.

When configuring your OSINT workspace, ensure that you have access to reliable and up-to-date sources of information. Familiarize yourself with authoritative websites, databases, and public records that are relevant to your OSINT objectives. Bookmark these sources or create a curated list of URLs for quick reference during your investigations.

Finally, consider the importance of ongoing training and skill development as part of your workspace configuration. OSINT is a dynamic field with constantly evolving tools and techniques. Stay updated by participating in OSINT communities, attending training sessions, and regularly practicing your skills to enhance your proficiency and effectiveness.

In summary, configuring the OSINT workspace is a crucial step in preparing for your open-source intelligence activities. A well-organized and secure environment, along with the right tools and workflows, will enhance your efficiency and effectiveness in collecting, analyzing, and managing OSINT data. By taking the time to configure your workspace thoughtfully, you can ensure that you are well-equipped to navigate the complex and dynamic landscape of open source information effectively.

Chapter 3: Metagoofil: Harvesting Metadata

To grasp the significance of metadata in the realm of open-source intelligence (OSINT) and information gathering, it is essential to delve into its nature and role. Metadata, often referred to as "data about data," is the contextual information associated with a piece of information or content. It serves as a descriptor that provides valuable insights into the origin, creation, and characteristics of the data it accompanies.

Metadata can take various forms, depending on the type of content it relates to. For example, in the context of digital images, metadata may include details such as the date and time the image was captured, the camera model used, GPS coordinates of the location, and even the photographer's name. In documents, metadata can encompass information about the author, creation date, editing history, and document properties.

Understanding metadata is essential for OSINT practitioners because it often holds concealed information that can be leveraged for investigative and analytical purposes. While the content of a document or file may be the primary focus, metadata provides valuable context that can aid in the verification, attribution, and analysis of the data.

One of the most common sources of metadata in the digital age is found in electronic files, particularly documents and images. These files often contain embedded metadata that can reveal a wealth of information. For instance, a PDF document may include metadata about the author, keywords, document title, and even comments and annotations made by previous users.

Metadata can be categorized into two main types: structural metadata and descriptive metadata. Structural metadata describes the organization and layout of data within a file or document. This type of metadata helps software applications understand the structure of the data and how it should be displayed or processed. Descriptive metadata, on the other hand, provides information about the content itself. It includes details such as titles, keywords, abstracts, and copyright information.

Metadata can be embedded within files using various standards and formats. For example, EXIF (Exchangeable Image File Format) metadata is commonly used in digital photographs. It stores information about the camera settings, date and time of capture, and even the device's serial number. In contrast, documents often contain metadata in formats like Dublin Core, which includes standardized elements for describing resources.

OSINT practitioners can harness the power of metadata to gain valuable insights in a variety of scenarios. For instance, during a digital forensic investigation, examining the metadata of a suspect's documents or images can help establish a timeline of events or verify the authenticity of evidence. In the context of journalism, verifying the authenticity and source of a document or image is crucial, and metadata can provide vital clues.

Metadata can also play a role in geospatial analysis. GPS coordinates embedded in photos or documents can reveal the precise location where the content was created. This information is valuable for mapping and tracking purposes, whether it's monitoring the movement of assets, verifying the location of a crime scene, or assessing the geographic distribution of social media posts.

In the realm of OSINT, understanding metadata is particularly relevant when it comes to online investigations.

Social media platforms, websites, and digital communication tools often strip away some metadata during data transfer, but they still retain valuable information. For instance, social media posts may include timestamps, geolocation data, and even user agent information that can be used to track the source or author of the content.

Metadata analysis becomes even more potent when combined with other OSINT techniques. For example, geolocation data from a photo can be cross-referenced with social media posts, IP address information, and other open-source data to build a comprehensive profile of an individual's activities and movements. This synergy of metadata with other OSINT methods can yield deeper insights and actionable intelligence.

Despite its immense potential, metadata analysis in the OSINT field is not without challenges. Some individuals and organizations are aware of the sensitivity of metadata and take measures to sanitize or remove it from files before sharing them online. Additionally, metadata can be manipulated or spoofed, making it important to verify its authenticity. Therefore, OSINT practitioners must exercise caution and corroborate their findings using multiple sources and methods.

In summary, metadata serves as a valuable source of contextual information in the world of open-source intelligence. Understanding metadata, its types, and its potential applications is essential for OSINT practitioners seeking to uncover hidden insights, verify information, and conduct investigations effectively. By integrating metadata analysis into their toolkit and combining it with other OSINT techniques, practitioners can unlock a deeper level of understanding in their pursuit of information and intelligence in the open domain.

To fully appreciate the practical usage of Metagoofil in open-source intelligence (OSINT) and information gathering, it is essential to understand its capabilities and how it can be applied effectively. Metagoofil is a powerful OSINT tool that specializes in the extraction of metadata from various types of documents, such as PDFs, Word documents, and Excel spreadsheets. This metadata often contains valuable information about the document's author, timestamps, software used, and potentially even sensitive details.

Metagoofil operates by parsing documents and extracting metadata from them, which can be invaluable for OSINT practitioners and investigators. One of the primary use cases of Metagoofil is in digital forensic investigations, where it helps analysts uncover hidden details within documents that may be relevant to a case. By extracting metadata, investigators can determine the origin and history of a document, potentially identifying the author or contributors.

Journalists and researchers also find Metagoofil to be a valuable tool in their work. When dealing with leaked documents or reports, analyzing metadata can help verify the authenticity of the content and identify any potential alterations or tampering. This is particularly crucial in cases involving sensitive information or whistleblowers.

The legal profession can benefit from Metagoofil as well. Attorneys and legal investigators can use the tool to examine documents for hidden information that may be relevant to a case, such as timestamps that establish the timeline of events or the source of the document. This can be critical in building a strong legal argument or presenting evidence in court.

Corporate investigations also make extensive use of Metagoofil. When conducting due diligence on a company or its employees, extracting metadata from documents can reveal important information about the organization's structure, key personnel, and document history. This can aid in risk assessment and decision-making during mergers, acquisitions, or partnerships.

In the field of cybersecurity, Metagoofil can play a vital role in identifying potential security risks. By analyzing the metadata of documents within an organization's network, security professionals can uncover sensitive information that may be inadvertently exposed, such as internal file paths, usernames, or software versions. This information can be used to strengthen security measures and protect against potential threats.

One of the key advantages of Metagoofil is its ability to analyze a wide range of document types, including PDFs, Word documents, and Excel spreadsheets. This versatility makes it a valuable tool for extracting metadata from various sources and formats, providing OSINT practitioners with flexibility in their investigations. Additionally, Metagoofil is relatively easy to use, making it accessible to both beginners and experienced professionals in the OSINT field.

To use Metagoofil effectively, OSINT practitioners typically provide the tool with a target domain or URL to search for documents. Metagoofil then scans the specified domain, retrieving documents it finds and extracting their metadata. This process can be automated, allowing for efficient data collection and analysis.

The extracted metadata can include information such as document titles, authors, creation dates, modification dates, software used, and more. Depending on the document, this metadata can provide valuable context and insights into the content's origin and history.

In practice, Metagoofil can be employed in various scenarios. For example, during an OSINT investigation of a company,

Metagoofil can be used to scan the organization's website and extract metadata from publicly available documents. This information may reveal details about the company's structure, employees, and internal processes.

In the realm of competitive intelligence, Metagoofil can assist businesses in analyzing metadata from their competitors' public documents. By examining metadata from reports, presentations, or product documentation, companies can gain insights into their rivals' strategies and capabilities.

Metagoofil can also be used in conjunction with other OSINT tools and techniques. For instance, when combined with social media monitoring or web scraping, it can provide a more comprehensive view of an individual or organization's online presence and activities. This synergy of OSINT methods can yield deeper insights and a more complete picture for intelligence gathering.

While Metagoofil is a powerful tool, it is essential for OSINT practitioners to use it responsibly and ethically. Respect for privacy and legal considerations should always guide its usage. Additionally, it's crucial to verify and cross-reference information obtained from metadata with other sources to ensure accuracy and reliability.

In summary, Metagoofil is a valuable asset in the OSINT toolkit, offering the capability to extract metadata from a variety of document types. Its practical usage spans across various fields, including digital forensics, journalism, law, corporate investigations, and cybersecurity. By harnessing Metagoofil's capabilities, OSINT practitioners can uncover hidden information, verify the authenticity of documents, and enhance their investigative and analytical efforts in the open-source intelligence domain.

Chapter 4: theHarvester: Gathering Email Intelligence

Email intelligence plays a pivotal role in the realm of open-source intelligence (OSINT), providing valuable insights into individuals, organizations, and their activities. Emails are a ubiquitous form of digital communication, and as such, they often contain a wealth of information that can be leveraged for investigative and analytical purposes. Understanding the nuances of email intelligence is essential for OSINT practitioners seeking to extract meaningful data from email sources.

Emails are a rich source of metadata, which includes information about the sender, recipient, subject, timestamps, and more. This metadata can reveal essential details about the communication's context, such as when an email was sent, who was involved, and the frequency of communication. Analyzing email metadata is a fundamental aspect of email intelligence, as it can provide valuable insights into an individual's or organization's behavior and relationships.

One of the primary use cases for email intelligence is in digital forensic investigations. Forensic analysts often examine email communication to reconstruct timelines, identify involved parties, and establish patterns of communication. This can be instrumental in cases involving cybercrimes, fraud, harassment, or other illegal activities. Email intelligence can help investigators trace the origins of malicious emails, track down cybercriminals, and gather evidence for legal proceedings.

Email intelligence is also valuable in the context of corporate investigations. When conducting due diligence on potential business partners or employees, organizations may analyze email communication to gain insights into an individual's professional network, affiliations, and past collaborations. By examining email metadata and content, companies can make informed decisions about their relationships and potential risks.

Journalists and researchers frequently utilize email intelligence in their work. When investigating stories or conducting research, journalists may analyze leaked emails to uncover hidden information, verify claims, or expose wrongdoing. Email metadata can be used to corroborate the authenticity of leaked documents and establish the timeline of events.

In the legal profession, email intelligence can be a critical tool for building cases and presenting evidence. Attorneys may use email communication as evidence in court, and email metadata can help establish the credibility and context of the messages. Legal investigators often analyze email communication to identify key witnesses, document conversations, and gather relevant information for legal proceedings.

The process of gathering email intelligence typically begins with the collection of emails from various sources. OSINT practitioners may obtain emails from publicly available datasets, online forums, social media platforms, or leaked databases. It's essential to respect legal and ethical boundaries when collecting email data and ensure compliance with data privacy regulations.

Once email data is acquired, the next step in email intelligence is the analysis of email metadata. This analysis involves extracting and examining information such as sender and recipient email addresses, subject lines, timestamps, and any other available metadata fields. Tools and techniques for parsing and organizing email metadata are often employed to streamline the process.

Analyzing email content is another crucial aspect of email intelligence. The body of an email can contain valuable information, including discussions, plans, and details about events or transactions. OSINT practitioners may use natural language processing (NLP) techniques to extract meaningful insights from email text. NLP can assist in identifying keywords, sentiment analysis, and topic modeling to uncover hidden patterns and trends within email content.

Email intelligence can also involve identifying email patterns and relationships. This includes mapping the communication networks of individuals or organizations. By examining who communicates with whom and the frequency of interactions, analysts can uncover affiliations, alliances, or dependencies. Social network analysis (SNA) techniques can be applied to visualize and analyze these relationships effectively.

Geolocation information can be extracted from email data as well. Email headers may contain IP addresses, which can be used to determine the geographical location of the sender or recipient. Geolocation data can be valuable in investigations related to cybercrimes, cyberattacks, or tracking the movements of individuals.

While email intelligence offers significant benefits, it is not without challenges. Privacy concerns and legal regulations must be considered when collecting and analyzing email data. OSINT practitioners must adhere to ethical guidelines and obtain consent when applicable. Moreover, email communication can be encrypted, making it challenging to access the content and metadata. In such cases, OSINT professionals may need to rely on other sources or methods to gather relevant information.

To enhance email intelligence capabilities, OSINT practitioners may utilize specialized tools and software designed for email analysis. These tools can streamline the extraction of metadata, facilitate content analysis, and assist in visualizing email relationships. Some email intelligence tools also offer automation features to handle large datasets efficiently.

In summary, email intelligence is a valuable component of open-source intelligence, providing insights into individuals, organizations, and their activities through the analysis of email data. From digital forensics to corporate investigations, journalism, and the legal profession, email intelligence plays a vital role in various fields. OSINT practitioners must navigate the complexities of email data collection and analysis while adhering to ethical and legal standards. By harnessing the power of email intelligence, investigators and analysts can uncover hidden information, verify claims, and make informed decisions in the pursuit of actionable intelligence.

To harness the power of theHarvester effectively in open-source intelligence (OSINT) and email data gathering, it is crucial to comprehend its functionality and practical applications. theHarvester is a versatile OSINT tool that specializes in collecting email addresses, subdomains, and other related information from various online sources. Email data can be a goldmine of intelligence, providing insights into an organization's structure, key personnel, and online presence.

The primary utility of theHarvester lies in its ability to automate the process of gathering email addresses and domain-related information. OSINT practitioners often use this tool to discover email addresses associated with a target domain or organization. This information can be invaluable for investigations, reconnaissance, and cybersecurity assessments.

One of the primary use cases for theHarvester is in cybersecurity and vulnerability assessments. Security professionals and penetration testers leverage theHarvester to identify potential attack vectors, such as email addresses that can be targeted for phishing campaigns. By discovering email addresses associated with a target, security teams can assess the organization's susceptibility to email-based attacks and take proactive measures to mitigate risks.

Digital forensics and incident response teams also find theHarvester to be a valuable asset in their investigations. During digital forensics examinations, analysts may need to collect email addresses and other domain-related data from an individual's or organization's online presence. This data can help trace the origin of digital artifacts and provide insights into communication patterns.

Journalists and investigative reporters frequently use theHarvester to uncover hidden information and sources. When conducting investigations, journalists may need to identify key individuals or sources within an organization. By collecting email addresses associated with the target domain, they can reach out to potential sources for interviews or comments.

In the field of competitive intelligence, theHarvester can aid businesses in gathering information about their competitors. Companies may use the tool to discover email addresses of key personnel, monitor changes in their online presence, and analyze their digital footprint. This data can be used to gain insights into competitors' strategies and activities.

To utilize theHarvester effectively, OSINT practitioners typically provide specific input parameters, including the target domain or organization, search sources, and the type of data to collect. theHarvester then queries various online resources and search engines to retrieve relevant information. The tool's modular design allows users to choose from multiple data sources, making it adaptable to various OSINT scenarios.

One of the critical functionalities of theHarvester is its ability to discover subdomains associated with a target domain. Subdomains are often used by organizations for different purposes, such as hosting web applications, blogs, or internal resources. Identifying subdomains can provide valuable insights into an organization's online infrastructure and potential attack surfaces.

theHarvester also excels at collecting email addresses from public sources, such as search engines, social media platforms, and public databases. These email addresses may be publicly available but scattered across different websites and sources. theHarvester automates the process of aggregating this data into a consolidated list for further analysis.

Another practical application of theHarvester is in domain reconnaissance. OSINT practitioners can use the tool to enumerate information about a target domain, such as its DNS records, MX (Mail Exchange) records, and associated IP addresses. This data can be useful for assessing an organization's online presence, email infrastructure, and potential vulnerabilities.

Email addresses collected by theHarvester can be further analyzed and validated using other OSINT techniques and tools. For instance, email addresses can be cross-referenced with social media profiles, online forums, or publicly available databases to verify their authenticity and gather additional information about individuals associated with those addresses.

While theHarvester is a valuable asset in the OSINT toolkit, it is essential for practitioners to use it responsibly and ethically. Respect for privacy and legal considerations should always guide its usage. Additionally, OSINT practitioners should be aware that email addresses collected by theHarvester may not always be up-to-date or accurate, as online information can change over time.

To enhance theHarvester's capabilities, OSINT practitioners may combine it with other OSINT tools and techniques. For example, email addresses collected by theHarvester can be used as input for email verification tools that validate the existence and deliverability of email addresses. This additional step ensures the accuracy of the collected data.

In summary, theHarvester is a versatile and powerful tool for gathering email addresses and domain-related information in the field of open-source intelligence. From cybersecurity assessments to digital forensics, journalism, and competitive intelligence, theHarvester finds applications across various domains. OSINT practitioners can leverage its automation capabilities to streamline data collection and analysis, ultimately enhancing their ability to uncover hidden information and make informed decisions in the open-source intelligence domain.

Chapter 5: Mitaka: Automating OSINT Tasks

To embark on a journey into the world of Mitaka automation in open-source intelligence (OSINT), it is essential to first grasp the significance and potential of this powerful tool. Mitaka is an OSINT automation and orchestration framework designed to simplify and enhance the efficiency of OSINT investigations. Automation has become increasingly crucial in the field of OSINT as the volume of available data continues to grow exponentially, making it challenging for analysts to manually collect, process, and analyze information effectively.

The core idea behind Mitaka automation is to streamline and automate repetitive and time-consuming tasks that OSINT practitioners encounter during their investigations. These tasks can range from gathering data from various online sources to processing and analyzing the collected information. By automating these processes, Mitaka allows analysts to focus their time and expertise on higher-level tasks, such as data interpretation, pattern recognition, and intelligence generation.

Mitaka's versatility is one of its standout features. It supports a wide range of OSINT tools and data sources, making it adaptable to various investigative scenarios. Whether you are conducting research on individuals, organizations, websites, or social media profiles, Mitaka can be tailored to your specific needs. This flexibility is essential in a rapidly evolving OSINT landscape where new tools and sources constantly emerge.

The automation capabilities of Mitaka extend to data collection, processing, and analysis. For instance, you can use Mitaka to automate the collection of data from multiple websites or social media platforms simultaneously. This is particularly valuable when monitoring online discussions, tracking trends, or conducting real-time investigations. Mitaka can extract text, images, and metadata from online content, providing a comprehensive view of the information landscape.

Data processing is another area where Mitaka excels. It can automate tasks such as data cleaning, normalization, and enrichment. For example, if you have a large dataset of social media posts, Mitaka can automatically remove duplicates, standardize date formats, and enhance the data with additional context, such as geolocation information or sentiment analysis scores. This automation significantly accelerates the preparation of data for analysis.

Mitaka's automation capabilities also extend to data analysis and visualization. It can generate reports, charts, and graphs based on the collected data, making it easier for analysts to identify patterns, trends, and anomalies. These visualizations aid in the interpretation of complex data and the communication of findings to stakeholders.

One of Mitaka's notable strengths is its integration with third-party OSINT tools and services. It can seamlessly connect with popular OSINT tools like Maltego, Shodan, and theHarvester, allowing you to leverage the capabilities of these tools within the Mitaka framework. This integration simplifies the process of accessing and utilizing diverse OSINT resources.

Mitaka automation is not limited to static data collection. It can also support dynamic data sources and real-time monitoring. For example, if you are interested in tracking social media mentions of a specific keyword or monitoring changes on a website, Mitaka can automate these tasks and provide timely updates. This real-time capability is essential for staying informed about rapidly evolving events or topics.

The automation scripts in Mitaka are written in Python, a widely used programming language in the field of OSINT. This allows OSINT practitioners to create custom automation scripts tailored to their specific requirements. Whether you need to automate interactions with an online platform, extract data from APIs, or implement advanced analysis techniques, Mitaka's extensibility empowers you to do so.

Another key feature of Mitaka is its support for collaboration and knowledge sharing among OSINT practitioners. It provides a platform for creating and sharing automation scripts, workflows, and best practices. This collaborative aspect fosters a community-driven approach to OSINT automation, where practitioners can learn from each other and collectively enhance their investigative capabilities.

To get started with Mitaka automation, you will need to install the framework on your system and configure it according to your needs. Mitaka provides extensive documentation and tutorials to guide you through the installation and setup process. Once configured, you can begin creating automation scripts or workflows using Mitaka's built-in functions and modules.

When designing automation workflows in Mitaka, it is essential to define clear objectives and requirements for your investigation. Consider the specific data sources you need to access, the tasks you want to automate, and the desired output format for your results. Planning your automation workflow in advance will help you maximize the efficiency and effectiveness of your OSINT activities.

Mitaka automation is not a one-size-fits-all solution, and its effectiveness depends on the quality of your automation scripts and the relevance of your chosen data sources. Therefore, it is crucial to continually evaluate and refine your automation workflows to ensure they align with your investigative goals and adapt to evolving OSINT challenges.

In summary, Mitaka automation represents a significant advancement in the field of open-source intelligence. Its ability to streamline data collection, processing, and analysis, coupled with its integration capabilities and extensibility, makes it a valuable tool for OSINT practitioners. By harnessing the power of Mitaka automation, analysts can enhance their efficiency, gain deeper insights from data, and stay ahead in the ever-changing landscape of open-source intelligence.

To navigate the realm of Mitaka automation effectively, it is essential to delve into the creation of Mitaka workflows and understand how they can optimize your open-source intelligence (OSINT) investigations. Mitaka workflows serve as a structured sequence of automated tasks, enabling OSINT practitioners to orchestrate and streamline the collection, processing, and analysis of data. Crafting efficient Mitaka workflows requires a thoughtful approach, careful planning, and a deep understanding of your investigative objectives.

The foundation of a Mitaka workflow begins with a clear definition of the investigative goal or problem you aim to solve. Whether you are conducting research on a specific target, monitoring a topic of interest, or tracking online discussions, a well-defined objective provides the essential framework for building your workflow.

With your investigative goal in mind, the next step is to identify the data sources that are relevant to your investigation. Mitaka offers a wide range of built-in data sources, including search engines, social media platforms, web scraping tools, and OSINT APIs. Additionally, Mitaka allows you to integrate third-party OSINT tools and services, expanding the scope of available data sources.

To create a Mitaka workflow, you'll need to decide which data sources to include and how to configure them. Each data source may require specific parameters, such as search queries, keywords, or user profiles. Carefully configuring these parameters ensures that your workflow retrieves the most relevant and targeted data.

One of the key advantages of Mitaka is its modularity, allowing you to build complex workflows by combining multiple tasks and data sources. Each task within a workflow represents a specific operation, such as data collection, data processing, analysis, or visualization. Tasks can be connected sequentially, forming a chain of automated actions that progress logically towards your investigative goal.

A well-structured Mitaka workflow typically begins with data collection tasks. These tasks gather data from selected sources, such as search engine queries, social media profiles, or websites. Mitaka's automation capabilities simplify the process of data retrieval, enabling you to efficiently collect information from diverse online platforms.

Once data collection tasks are configured, Mitaka can automate the execution of these tasks, saving you time and effort. Automated data collection ensures that your workflow consistently acquires the latest information from the chosen sources, reducing the risk of missing critical updates or changes.

After collecting data, the next step in your Mitaka workflow may involve data processing tasks. Data processing tasks are responsible for cleaning, normalizing, and enriching the collected data. These tasks ensure that the data is in a consistent format and ready for analysis. Mitaka provides built-in functions and modules to perform various data processing operations, such as text extraction, date standardization, and geolocation tagging.

Data analysis tasks play a pivotal role in Mitaka workflows. These tasks are responsible for extracting insights and intelligence from the collected and processed data. Mitaka offers various analysis modules, including natural language processing (NLP), sentiment analysis, keyword extraction, and topic modeling. By incorporating these tasks into your workflow, you can uncover hidden patterns, trends, and actionable information within the data.

Visualization tasks can be integrated into your Mitaka workflow to enhance data interpretation and communication. Visualization tools and libraries, such as Matplotlib or Plotly, can be used to create charts, graphs, and interactive visualizations based on the analyzed data. Visual representations simplify complex data and facilitate the communication of findings to stakeholders.

Mitaka workflows can also include tasks for real-time monitoring and alerts. These tasks enable you to track specific data sources continuously and receive notifications when predefined conditions or events occur. Real-time monitoring is particularly valuable for staying informed about rapidly evolving situations or trends.

When designing Mitaka workflows, consider the frequency of data collection and analysis tasks. Depending on your investigative objectives, you may configure tasks to run periodically, such as daily, weekly, or in real-time. Frequent data updates ensure that your workflow remains up-to-date and responsive to changing circumstances.

Mitaka's extensibility allows you to create custom automation scripts and modules tailored to your specific requirements. If Mitaka's built-in tasks and modules do not fully address your needs, you can develop custom code to extend its functionality. This capability empowers you to adapt Mitaka to unique OSINT challenges and investigative scenarios.

To build Mitaka workflows effectively, it is essential to test and validate each component thoroughly. Testing helps identify potential issues, such as data collection errors or misconfigured tasks, before deploying your workflow in a live investigation. Mitaka provides debugging and testing tools to facilitate this process.

Documentation is a crucial aspect of Mitaka workflow development. Properly documenting your workflow, including task configurations, data sources, and parameters, ensures that your workflow can be understood and maintained by other OSINT practitioners or collaborators. Clear documentation also aids in troubleshooting and troubleshooting issues that may arise during workflow execution.

Mitaka workflows can be stored and shared as code repositories, allowing other OSINT practitioners to access and benefit from your automation scripts. This collaborative approach fosters knowledge sharing and accelerates the development of automation solutions within the OSINT community.

In summary, creating Mitaka workflows is a strategic process that empowers OSINT practitioners to automate and optimize their investigative efforts. With careful planning, well-defined objectives, and an understanding of available data sources, Mitaka workflows can streamline data collection, processing, analysis, and visualization. By harnessing the power of Mitaka automation, analysts can enhance their efficiency, extract meaningful insights from data, and excel in the ever-evolving landscape of open-source intelligence.

Chapter 6: BuiltWith: Profiling Website Technologies

Website profiling holds a pivotal role in the realm of open-source intelligence (OSINT), serving as a potent technique for extracting valuable information about websites, organizations, and individuals. In the digital age, websites are a fundamental element of an entity's online presence, representing a gateway to its activities, affiliations, and digital footprint. Understanding the significance of website profiling is essential for OSINT practitioners seeking to harness the power of this technique to gather intelligence effectively.

At its core, website profiling encompasses the systematic examination and analysis of websites to extract pertinent details about their structure, technologies, content, and potential vulnerabilities. Websites are dynamic entities that can reveal a wealth of information, ranging from the technologies they employ to the individuals or organizations behind them.

One of the primary objectives of website profiling is to identify the technologies and software frameworks that power a website. This includes detecting the web server software, content management systems (CMS), programming languages, and third-party plugins or extensions used on the site. Understanding the technology stack of a website provides insights into its security posture, potential vulnerabilities, and the level of sophistication of its operators.

Website profiling also involves the extraction of metadata associated with web pages. Metadata includes information such as page titles, authorship details, keywords, and timestamps. This metadata can be invaluable in understanding the context and purpose of web content, as well as identifying individuals or organizations responsible for its creation.

Profiling a website often extends to mapping its structure and content hierarchy. This includes identifying the site's directory structure, internal links, and the organization of web pages. Analyzing the layout and organization of a website can reveal its underlying objectives, content priorities, and navigation patterns.

Website profiling techniques can help OSINT practitioners discover hidden or sensitive directories and files that are not readily visible through standard website navigation. By uncovering these hidden resources, analysts may stumble upon valuable information, such as confidential documents, databases, or administrative interfaces that were not meant to be public.

Moreover, website profiling plays a crucial role in tracking the digital footprint of individuals, organizations, or threat actors. Websites are often associated with domain names, IP addresses, and hosting providers. Profiling these aspects can help establish connections between different online entities and uncover affiliations, ownership, or patterns of behavior.

In the context of cybersecurity and threat intelligence, website profiling aids in identifying potentially malicious websites or domains. OSINT practitioners can use profiling techniques to assess the legitimacy and reputation of websites, checking for signs of phishing, malware distribution, or other malicious activities. Profiling also assists in tracking the infrastructure used by cybercriminals and threat actors.

Competitive intelligence and market research benefit from website profiling as well. Organizations can analyze the online presence of competitors, identifying their website technologies, digital marketing strategies, and customer engagement tactics. This information can inform business strategies and help companies stay competitive in their respective industries.

For digital marketing and SEO (Search Engine Optimization) professionals, website profiling is instrumental in evaluating the performance of websites in terms of search engine rankings, site speed, and user experience. Profiling tools can assess factors such as page load times, mobile-friendliness, and the presence of structured data, offering insights into areas for improvement.

Website profiling is not limited to public websites; it extends to dark web and hidden services as well. OSINT practitioners may use specialized techniques and tools to profile websites hosted on the dark web, identifying potential sources of illicit activities, marketplaces, or underground forums. Profiling hidden services is crucial for tracking criminal networks and monitoring emerging threats.

To conduct effective website profiling, OSINT practitioners rely on a combination of automated tools, manual analysis, and investigative techniques. Automated tools can quickly scan websites, extract metadata, and identify technologies, streamlining the profiling process. Manual analysis, on the other hand, allows analysts to dive deeper into website content, structure, and contextual clues.

Website profiling can be initiated by analyzing the HTTP response headers of a website, which often contain valuable information about the server software and technologies in use. Tools like Wappalyzer or BuiltWith can automatically detect and report on the technologies detected in HTTP headers, providing a quick overview of a website's tech stack.

Another important aspect of website profiling is DNS (Domain Name System) analysis. This involves examining domain registration records, WHOIS data, and DNS records to gather information about domain ownership, registration history, and related domains. OSINT practitioners can use tools like WHOIS databases and domain reputation services to aid in this analysis.

Web scraping techniques are commonly employed in website profiling to extract specific data from web pages. By scripting custom web scrapers or using scraping tools, analysts can collect information such as contact details, product listings, or news articles from websites. This data can be used for various OSINT purposes, including market research and competitive analysis.

Web archive services like the Wayback Machine enable OSINT practitioners to access historical snapshots of websites, allowing them to track changes over time and retrieve content that may have been removed or altered. This historical context can be valuable for investigations and research.

Website profiling also extends to social media platforms and online forums where individuals and organizations maintain a digital presence. OSINT practitioners can profile social media profiles, extracting information about user activity, connections, and engagement. Analyzing online discussions and posts can provide insights into an entity's interests, affiliations, and opinions.

In summary, website profiling is a fundamental technique in open-source intelligence, offering valuable insights into websites, organizations, and individuals. It encompasses the analysis of website technologies, metadata, content, structure, and affiliations. OSINT practitioners use profiling to gather intelligence, assess cybersecurity risks, track digital footprints, conduct competitive analysis, and uncover hidden or malicious online activities. Leveraging automated tools, manual analysis, and investigative techniques, website profiling is a versatile and indispensable skill in the arsenal of OSINT professionals.

To truly harness the power of BuiltWith in open-source intelligence (OSINT), one must delve into the realm of in-depth analysis, a process that enables OSINT practitioners to extract comprehensive insights from the technology profiles of websites and online platforms. BuiltWith is a versatile tool designed to identify and analyze the technologies, frameworks, and components underpinning a website's infrastructure. This in-depth analysis not only provides valuable technical information but also sheds light on an organization's digital strategies, potential vulnerabilities, and competitive landscape.

At the core of BuiltWith's capabilities is its ability to uncover the technology stack of a website. This includes identifying the web server software, content management systems (CMS), programming languages, databases, analytics tools, marketing platforms, and various third-party components. Knowing the technology stack empowers OSINT practitioners with a deeper understanding of a website's architecture and its operational framework.

BuiltWith excels in unveiling the presence of e-commerce solutions on websites. It can identify e-commerce platforms, payment gateways, shopping cart systems, and other related tools. This insight is invaluable for competitive analysis, as it allows organizations to gain a better understanding of their competitors' e-commerce strategies, product offerings, and customer engagement methods.

Another significant aspect of BuiltWith's analysis capabilities is its ability to detect marketing and advertising technologies used by a website. This includes tracking pixels, ad networks, email marketing platforms, social media integration, and more. By identifying a website's marketing stack, OSINT practitioners can gain insights into its digital marketing strategies, advertising partnerships, and customer acquisition channels.

BuiltWith's analysis extends to content management systems, a critical component of many websites. It can identify popular CMS platforms such as WordPress, Joomla, Drupal, or custom-built systems. Understanding the CMS used by a website is essential for assessing its content management capabilities, customization potential, and potential security vulnerabilities associated with the platform.

In-depth analysis with BuiltWith includes the identification of analytics and tracking tools employed by websites. This involves detecting the presence of Google Analytics, Adobe Analytics, or other analytics solutions. Knowledge of these tools provides insights into a website's data collection practices, audience segmentation, and performance tracking.

BuiltWith also offers insights into a website's hosting infrastructure. It can identify hosting providers, IP addresses, and server locations. This information can be useful for understanding the hosting choices made by an organization, potential server vulnerabilities, and geographical targeting strategies.

Furthermore, BuiltWith can uncover the use of security technologies, including SSL certificates, firewalls, and content delivery networks (CDNs). These insights are vital for assessing a website's security posture and its readiness to protect against cyber threats and attacks.

The analysis with BuiltWith delves into tracking the presence of widgets and plugins. It can identify third-party integrations and extensions, such as social media sharing buttons, chatbots, and customer support tools. This knowledge is critical for evaluating a website's user experience, functionality, and the extent to which it relies on external services.

BuiltWith's extensive analysis capabilities also encompass the detection of advertising and affiliate networks. This includes identifying ad platforms, affiliate marketing programs, and associated tracking codes. Understanding a website's monetization strategies and partnerships can be valuable for competitive analysis and business intelligence.

In addition to identifying technologies, BuiltWith provides historical data about technology changes on websites. This historical context allows OSINT practitioners to track technology stack modifications, content updates, and platform migrations over time. It can reveal insights into an organization's evolving digital strategies and priorities.

Moreover, BuiltWith offers insights into mobile app integration, including the presence of mobile application components and software development kits (SDKs). This knowledge can be instrumental for organizations exploring mobile marketing strategies or assessing mobile app adoption by competitors.

BuiltWith analysis can be used for competitive intelligence, benchmarking an organization's digital presence against industry peers or rivals. By comparing technology stacks, marketing tools, and strategies, businesses can gain a competitive edge and identify areas for improvement.

For cybersecurity professionals, in-depth analysis with BuiltWith can aid in identifying potential attack vectors and vulnerabilities associated with the technology stack of a website. Vulnerabilities in web server software, CMS platforms, or third-party plugins can be assessed and addressed proactively.

Additionally, BuiltWith's analysis capabilities can assist organizations in compliance and risk management. By identifying third-party data processors, tracking technologies, and privacy-related components, businesses can ensure compliance with data protection regulations and assess the privacy implications of using specific web services. To conduct an in-depth analysis with BuiltWith, OSINT practitioners start by inputting the target website's URL into the tool. BuiltWith then generates a comprehensive report detailing the technologies and components detected on the website. This report can be further customized to focus on specific aspects, such as e-commerce platforms, analytics tools, or advertising networks.

Once the analysis report is generated, OSINT practitioners can explore the detected technologies in detail. BuiltWith provides additional information about each technology, including vendor details, popularity, and usage statistics. This level of granularity enables practitioners to assess the significance of each technology within the website's infrastructure.

Furthermore, BuiltWith allows users to export analysis reports in various formats, making it convenient to share findings with colleagues or stakeholders. The tool also offers integration options with other OSINT tools and platforms, facilitating seamless information sharing and analysis workflows.

In summary, in-depth analysis with BuiltWith is a valuable technique in the field of open-source intelligence. It provides a comprehensive view of a website's technology stack, infrastructure, and digital strategies. OSINT practitioners can leverage this analysis to gain insights into organizations, assess their competitive landscape, evaluate cybersecurity risks, and make informed decisions in an increasingly digital world. By harnessing the power of BuiltWith, analysts can uncover hidden details and intelligence that may not be apparent on the surface of websites and online platforms.

Chapter 7: Social Media Investigations

To effectively harness the potential of social media in open-source intelligence (OSINT), it is imperative to comprehend the multifaceted role that social media platforms play in the digital landscape. Social media has evolved into a powerhouse of information, providing a wealth of publicly accessible data that can be leveraged for intelligence gathering, investigations, threat assessment, and more.

At its core, social media consists of online platforms where individuals, organizations, and communities share thoughts, opinions, images, videos, and personal information. These platforms include giants like Facebook, Twitter, Instagram, LinkedIn, YouTube, TikTok, and a plethora of others, each catering to specific user demographics and content types.

One of the primary advantages of social media for OSINT is its wealth of user-generated content. People routinely share personal experiences, activities, and opinions on these platforms, offering insights into their lives, interests, and affiliations. This voluntary disclosure of information provides OSINT practitioners with a rich source of data for analysis.

Social media platforms facilitate the creation of user profiles, each containing a trove of information about individuals or organizations. These profiles often include details such as names, usernames, profile pictures, biographical information, locations, contact information, and links to other online profiles. OSINT practitioners can gather and analyze this information to build comprehensive profiles of their subjects.

The content shared on social media extends beyond text-based posts. Users frequently upload images and videos, allowing OSINT practitioners to extract valuable metadata, such as geolocation, timestamps, and device information. This metadata can be used to track the movement and activities of individuals or identify the origins of multimedia content.

Hashtags, mentions, and keywords play a pivotal role in organizing and categorizing content on social media platforms. OSINT practitioners can monitor these elements to track discussions, trends, and relevant conversations related to specific topics, events, or entities. This real-time monitoring capability is particularly useful for staying updated on breaking news, emerging threats, and public sentiment.

Location-based information is a powerful aspect of social media OSINT. Many users voluntarily share their current or past locations, allowing practitioners to track movements, identify travel patterns, and associate individuals with specific geographic areas. Geotagged posts and check-ins provide valuable geospatial data for analysis.

The connections and relationships formed on social media platforms can be a goldmine of intelligence. OSINT practitioners can explore an individual's network of friends, followers, connections, or subscribers to uncover affiliations, associations, and potential sources of information. Examining the interactions and communications within these networks can reveal valuable insights.

Analyzing user activity patterns on social media can help OSINT practitioners identify routines, behaviors, and preferences. This information can be leveraged to predict future actions, interests, or potential vulnerabilities. For instance, monitoring an individual's posting habits may reveal predictable times of inactivity, which can be exploited for investigative purposes.

Sentiment analysis is a powerful tool in social media OSINT. By analyzing the tone, language, and sentiment expressed in posts and comments, practitioners can gauge public sentiment, opinions, and reactions to specific events or topics. This analysis can be valuable for assessing public perception and potential reputational risks.

Social media OSINT extends to the monitoring of events, gatherings, and protests. Users often share real-time updates, photos, and videos from these events, offering valuable insights into crowd sizes, locations, and participant demographics. Monitoring event-related hashtags and geotagged posts can aid in event assessment and situational awareness.

Verification and validation of information are crucial in social media OSINT. Not all information shared on social media is accurate or reliable. OSINT practitioners must employ techniques to corroborate data, cross-reference multiple sources, and assess the credibility of the information before drawing conclusions or making decisions based on it.

The importance of privacy settings on social media cannot be overstated. While much of the data on these platforms is publicly accessible, some users may have restricted their profiles to limit the visibility of their content. OSINT practitioners must respect privacy settings and only gather information that is publicly available.

To conduct effective social media OSINT, practitioners employ a combination of manual techniques and automated tools. Manual techniques involve browsing profiles, reading posts, and analyzing content to gather insights and make observations. Automated tools, on the other hand, can assist in data collection, monitoring, sentiment analysis, and network analysis.

Data collection tools, such as social media scrapers and crawlers, can help OSINT practitioners gather large volumes of data from social media platforms. These tools can extract posts, comments, user profiles, and multimedia content for further analysis. However, it is essential to use such tools in compliance with platform terms of service and legal regulations.

Monitoring tools and dashboards allow OSINT practitioners to track specific keywords, hashtags, or user accounts in real-time. These tools provide notifications and alerts when relevant content is posted, enabling practitioners to stay updated on developments related to their investigations or areas of interest.

Sentiment analysis tools employ natural language processing (NLP) techniques to assess the sentiment, emotions, and opinions expressed in social media content. These tools can help practitioners gauge public sentiment and identify trends or shifts in sentiment related to specific topics or entities.

Network analysis tools aid in visualizing and understanding the connections between individuals or organizations on social media platforms. These tools create graphical representations of social networks, showing relationships, interactions, and influential users. Network analysis can be instrumental in identifying key players and their roles in online communities.

Geospatial analysis tools allow OSINT practitioners to map and visualize geolocation data extracted from social media posts and images. Mapping geotagged content can help track movements, assess location-based trends, and identify patterns of activity.

To harness the wealth of information available on social media for open-source intelligence (OSINT) purposes, one must become proficient in various techniques for extracting social media data. Social media platforms host a diverse range of content, from text-based posts and comments to images, videos, and multimedia content, making the extraction process multifaceted and dynamic.

One fundamental technique for extracting social media data is manual data collection. This method involves navigating social media platforms, accessing user profiles, and manually copying or noting relevant information. OSINT practitioners can view public posts, comments, user profiles, and connections, gathering data directly from the platform's interface.

Another manual technique involves using advanced search features offered by some social media platforms. These features allow practitioners to narrow down search results by specifying keywords, hashtags, user accounts, dates, and other criteria. By refining search queries, practitioners can target specific content or discussions relevant to their investigations.

Social media APIs (Application Programming Interfaces) are powerful tools for extracting data programmatically. APIs provide structured access to social media platforms, enabling practitioners to retrieve data in a structured format, such as JSON or XML. This method allows for automated data collection and is suitable for handling large volumes of data efficiently.

Web scraping is a versatile technique used to extract data from social media platforms and websites. OSINT practitioners can develop web scraping scripts or use specialized tools to extract text, images, and other content from web pages. However, it's essential to be mindful of website terms of service and platform policies when scraping data.

Another valuable technique for extracting social media data is utilizing third-party data analytics and monitoring platforms. These platforms aggregate data from various social media sources, providing OSINT practitioners with comprehensive insights and visualizations. Some platforms offer sentiment analysis, keyword tracking, and real-time monitoring features.

Hashtag tracking tools are specialized tools designed to monitor and analyze hashtag usage on social media platforms. These tools allow practitioners to track the popularity and reach of specific hashtags, identify trending topics, and gauge public sentiment associated with them.

Image and video analysis tools employ machine learning and computer vision techniques to extract information from multimedia content shared on social media. These tools can identify objects, faces, logos, text, and other visual elements within images and videos. They are valuable for content analysis and identifying relevant metadata.

Geospatial data extraction tools are essential for collecting location-based information from social media. Geotagged posts and images often contain latitude and longitude coordinates, which can be mapped to visualize user locations and movements. Geospatial data is particularly useful for tracking events, emergencies, and activities in specific geographic areas.

Text analysis tools, including natural language processing (NLP) libraries and sentiment analysis algorithms, assist in processing and extracting insights from textual content shared on social media. These tools can identify sentiment, extract keywords, and detect trends within text-based posts and comments.

Network analysis tools visualize and analyze the connections between users, organizations, or entities on social media platforms. These tools create graphical representations of social networks, showcasing relationships, interactions, and influential users. Network analysis is instrumental for understanding the structure of online communities and identifying key actors.

Timeline analysis tools help OSINT practitioners track and analyze changes over time within social media data. These tools allow users to create timelines, identify trends, and visualize the evolution of discussions, events, or topics on social media platforms.

When extracting social media data, it's essential to consider ethical and legal implications. Privacy concerns, terms of service agreements, and platform policies must be respected. Practitioners should only collect publicly available information and refrain from invasive or unauthorized data collection methods.

Additionally, data verification and validation are crucial aspects of social media data extraction. Practitioners must cross-reference data from multiple sources, verify the authenticity of user accounts, and assess the credibility of information to ensure the accuracy of their findings.

Collaboration and information sharing within the OSINT community are valuable when working with social media data. OSINT practitioners often share techniques, tools, and best practices for data extraction and analysis, fostering a collaborative environment for knowledge exchange.

In summary, mastering techniques for extracting social media data is essential for OSINT practitioners seeking to leverage the vast and dynamic information landscape of social media platforms. Manual data collection, advanced search features, APIs, web scraping, third-party analytics platforms, and specialized tools play a crucial role in gathering and analyzing social media data. Practitioners must consider ethical, legal, and privacy considerations while extracting and using data from social media sources. By employing these techniques effectively, OSINT professionals can uncover valuable insights, monitor trends, and gather intelligence from the ever-expanding world of social media.

Chapter 8: Geolocation and Mapping

To delve into the fundamentals of geolocation in open-source intelligence (OSINT), one must recognize its pivotal role in extracting valuable location-based information from various sources and data points. Geolocation is the process of determining the physical location or geographic coordinates of an object, person, device, or event using different techniques and data sources.

The concept of geolocation revolves around the fundamental understanding of latitude and longitude, which are the two primary coordinates used to represent locations on the Earth's surface. Latitude measures how far north or south of the equator a point is, while longitude measures how far east or west it is from the Prime Meridian, which passes through Greenwich, England.

In OSINT, geolocation serves as a crucial technique for pinpointing the geographic origin or physical presence of individuals, organizations, or events. It plays a pivotal role in investigations, threat assessments, emergency response, and various intelligence-gathering tasks.

One of the primary sources of geolocation data in OSINT is metadata embedded in digital files, such as photos and videos. Most modern smartphones and digital cameras tag media files with geolocation information, including GPS coordinates, when capturing images or recording videos. This geotagged metadata can reveal the precise location where the media was created, offering valuable context and insights.

Web-based social media platforms are prolific sources of geolocation data. Users often voluntarily share their locations when posting content or checking in at specific places. Geolocation tags and check-ins provide valuable information about user movements, activities, and affiliations. Monitoring social media platforms for geotagged posts and check-ins is a common practice in OSINT.

Geolocation data is also extracted from internet infrastructure, including IP addresses and domain names. IP addresses can be mapped to geographic locations using databases that associate IP ranges with specific regions or cities. This information helps OSINT practitioners determine the approximate location of servers, websites, or online services.

Wi-Fi networks and cellular towers play a significant role in mobile device geolocation. Mobile devices constantly scan for available Wi-Fi networks and cellular towers, allowing location-based services to estimate their positions. These techniques, known as Wi-Fi positioning and cell tower triangulation, provide approximate location data for devices within range of these networks.

Geolocation is not limited to digital sources; it extends to physical evidence and human intelligence as well. OSINT practitioners often analyze physical clues, such as street signs, landmarks, and environmental features, visible in images or videos to infer location. Additionally, information gathered from human sources, witnesses, or informants can contribute to geolocation efforts.

Commercial geolocation services and mapping platforms, such as Google Maps, provide tools and APIs that facilitate geolocation tasks. These services allow OSINT practitioners to input coordinates, addresses, or landmarks to obtain geographic information, view maps, and perform reverse geocoding to determine the nearest known location based on coordinates.

Aerial and satellite imagery is another valuable resource for geolocation in OSINT. Services like Google Earth and satellite imagery providers offer high-resolution images that can help verify and analyze geographical features, structures, and locations of interest. Satellite imagery can also assist in monitoring remote or inaccessible areas.

When conducting geolocation tasks in OSINT, practitioners must consider the accuracy and precision of the data sources used. GPS coordinates from mobile devices or geotagged media can provide highly accurate location data. In contrast, IP address-based geolocation and Wi-Fi positioning may offer varying levels of accuracy, depending on factors like network density and the quality of location databases.

In some cases, geolocation efforts may involve reverse image search techniques. By uploading an image to search engines or specialized tools, OSINT practitioners can identify similar or matching images online. This process can help uncover additional context or find the original source of an image, which may include geolocation information.

Social media platforms often offer geolocation features that allow users to tag their current or past locations when posting content. Practitioners can search for posts, photos, or videos tagged with specific locations or landmarks, helping them gather location-based intelligence.

Geolocation in OSINT can also involve the analysis of historical data to track movements or events over time. Historical data, such as geotagged social media posts or archived satellite imagery, enables practitioners to create timelines and visualize changes in locations or activities.

Another critical aspect of geolocation in OSINT is the use of geospatial analysis tools and geographic information systems (GIS). These tools provide capabilities for mapping, spatial analysis, and data visualization. OSINT practitioners can overlay geolocation data onto maps, create heatmaps, and perform spatial queries to gain deeper insights into geographical patterns and trends.

Furthermore, OSINT practitioners can leverage geolocation data to assess and analyze events, incidents, or emergencies in real time. Monitoring social media platforms, news sources, and emergency services for geotagged content can help organizations respond swiftly to crises and coordinate resources effectively.

Ethical considerations are paramount when conducting geolocation in OSINT. Practitioners must respect privacy, data protection regulations, and platform policies. Gathering geolocation data from sources that explicitly prohibit its use for OSINT or investigative purposes may have legal implications.

In summary, the basics of geolocation in open-source intelligence encompass the understanding and utilization of geographic coordinates, metadata, digital sources, and physical evidence to determine the location of individuals, organizations, or events. Geolocation data is drawn from various sources, including geotagged media, IP addresses, Wi-Fi networks, cellular towers, commercial services, and human intelligence. OSINT practitioners employ tools and techniques to extract, analyze, and visualize geolocation data, helping them uncover valuable insights, track movements, and assess events in real time. Ethical and legal considerations are integral to responsible geolocation practices in OSINT, ensuring compliance with privacy and data protection regulations.

Mapping OSINT findings is a crucial step in the intelligence-gathering process, as it transforms disparate pieces of information into a visual representation that enhances comprehension and aids decision-making. Effective mapping enables OSINT practitioners to create a coherent narrative, identify patterns, and uncover relationships within the collected data.

To begin mapping OSINT findings, practitioners must first select appropriate mapping tools or software that align with their specific needs and objectives. Numerous mapping platforms are available, ranging from geographic information systems (GIS) software to web-based mapping applications and even open-source options.

One of the primary advantages of mapping OSINT findings is the ability to visualize geolocation data accurately. This includes mapping GPS coordinates, geotagged media, and location-based information extracted from various sources. By overlaying this data onto maps, practitioners gain a geographical context that enhances their understanding of events or subjects of interest.

Geospatial analysis tools within mapping software enable practitioners to perform spatial queries, such as proximity searches, buffer zones, and distance measurements. These tools facilitate the identification of locations within a specified radius, helping practitioners assess the spatial relationships between OSINT findings.

When mapping OSINT findings, practitioners often use geographic layers and overlays to display additional context. These layers can include administrative boundaries, infrastructure details, topography, and demographic information. Integrating such layers into the map can provide a broader perspective and facilitate deeper analysis.

One common approach to mapping OSINT findings is creating timelines that track the evolution of events or activities over time. Practitioners can use timeline visualization tools to display the chronological order of OSINT data, helping them identify trends, patterns, and historical context.

Network analysis is another valuable aspect of mapping OSINT findings. Practitioners can visualize connections and relationships between individuals, organizations, or entities using network mapping tools. This technique is particularly useful for uncovering hidden connections and understanding the structure of online communities.

Heatmaps are a powerful visualization tool in OSINT mapping. Heatmaps display the density of OSINT findings within a specific area, highlighting areas of high activity or concentration. This technique can assist practitioners in identifying hotspots, trends, and areas of interest.

Map annotations and labels are essential for providing context and additional information about OSINT findings. Practitioners can add markers, symbols, text labels, and notes to the map to explain key details or highlight significant findings. These annotations enhance the map's interpretability.

When mapping OSINT findings, practitioners should consider the intended audience and purpose of the map. Maps can be tailored to meet the needs of different stakeholders, whether they are law enforcement agencies, intelligence analysts, or decision-makers. Customizing map visualizations ensures that they effectively convey the relevant information.

Geospatial intelligence (GEOINT) techniques can complement OSINT mapping efforts. GEOINT involves the analysis of geospatial data from various sources, including satellite imagery, aerial photographs, and sensor data. Integrating GEOINT into OSINT mapping can provide additional layers of information and enhance situational awareness.

Advanced mapping platforms offer collaborative features that facilitate information sharing and teamwork among OSINT practitioners. These platforms allow multiple users to work on the same map simultaneously, share annotations, and collaborate on data analysis. Collaborative mapping is particularly valuable in complex investigations or intelligence operations.

In addition to visualizing geolocation data, OSINT practitioners can use mapping to analyze other types of OSINT findings. Text-based data, such as social media posts, news articles, and reports, can be geocoded to identify locations mentioned in the text. This process enables the creation of location-based word clouds or sentiment analysis maps.

When mapping OSINT findings, practitioners should pay attention to data accuracy and validation. Geolocation data should be cross-referenced with multiple sources to ensure its reliability. Incorrect or misleading data can lead to erroneous conclusions and misinformed decisions.

Ethical considerations are essential when mapping OSINT findings, especially if the data involves personally identifiable information (PII) or sensitive details. Practitioners must adhere to privacy regulations and ethical standards, ensuring that data handling and mapping practices respect individual rights and legal constraints.

Mapping OSINT findings is not limited to static maps; interactive maps can offer dynamic exploration capabilities. Interactive maps allow users to zoom in, pan, click on markers for additional information, and apply filters to focus on specific aspects of the data. These maps can be valuable tools for in-depth analysis and exploration.

Geographic analysis tools within mapping software enable practitioners to perform geospatial calculations, such as area measurements, route planning, and spatial statistics. These tools support a wide range of analytical tasks and can assist in deriving insights from geospatial data.

One critical aspect of mapping OSINT findings is the ability to update and adapt maps as new information becomes available. OSINT practitioners should regularly revisit and revise their maps to reflect the evolving nature of their investigations or intelligence tasks. This iterative process ensures that maps remain accurate and relevant.

In summary, mapping OSINT findings is a valuable technique that enhances the visualization, analysis, and interpretation of open-source intelligence data. Effective mapping provides practitioners with a spatial context, enabling them to uncover patterns, relationships, and insights within the collected information. OSINT practitioners can leverage various mapping tools, geospatial analysis techniques, and visualization methods to create informative and actionable maps tailored to their specific needs. Ethical considerations, data accuracy, and collaboration are integral aspects of successful OSINT mapping practices, ensuring that maps are used responsibly and effectively to support decision-making and investigations.

Chapter 9: Advanced Search Techniques

In the realm of open-source intelligence (OSINT), the ability to conduct precise and targeted searches is essential for uncovering valuable information and insights, and to achieve that, one must explore advanced search operators. These operators, often available through search engines and databases, provide powerful tools for refining queries and retrieving specific results.

The first advanced search operator to explore is the "site" operator, which allows users to restrict search results to a specific website or domain. By using "site:" followed by the website's URL, OSINT practitioners can focus their searches on a particular source, such as a government website, news outlet, or social media platform.

For example, searching for "site:cdc.gov COVID-19 guidelines" would yield results only from the Centers for Disease Control and Prevention's website, providing authoritative information on COVID-19 guidelines.

Another valuable search operator is "intitle," which enables users to find web pages with specific words or phrases in the page's title. By using "intitle:" followed by keywords, OSINT practitioners can locate web pages that are likely to contain information related to their query.

For instance, a search for "intitle:cybersecurity best practices" would return results with web pages that have "cybersecurity" and "best practices" in their titles.

The "inurl" operator is useful for finding web pages with specific words or phrases in the URL. It allows OSINT practitioners to target websites or directories that are likely to contain relevant information.

A search using "inurl:" followed by a keyword like "vulnerability" might lead to results containing URLs that include the term "vulnerability," helping identify web pages related to cybersecurity vulnerabilities.

The "filetype" operator allows users to search for specific types of files based on their extensions. This operator can be invaluable for finding documents, presentations, spreadsheets, and other file types relevant to an OSINT investigation.

For instance, using "filetype:pdf" followed by keywords like "annual report" could yield PDF documents of annual reports from various organizations.

OSINT practitioners can also employ the "related" operator to discover websites that are related to a specified URL. By entering "related:" followed by a web address, users can uncover websites that share similar content or themes.

For example, "related:example.com" might reveal websites that have content related to the example.com domain, potentially expanding the scope of research.

The "link" operator can be a valuable tool for finding web pages that link to a specific URL. By using "link:" followed by a web address, OSINT practitioners can identify pages that reference or cite a particular source.

A search with "link:wikipedia.org" could reveal web pages that link to Wikipedia articles, providing insights into the sources that reference Wikipedia's content.

To search for content that appears within a specific range of numbers, OSINT practitioners can employ the ".. " operator. This operator allows users to specify a numerical range, and the search engine will return results within that range.

For instance, searching for "price range $500..$1000" could help find products or services falling within that price range.

Boolean operators, such as "AND," "OR," and "NOT," enable users to combine keywords and operators to create complex search queries. "AND" narrows results by requiring both terms to appear, "OR" broadens results by including either term, and "NOT" excludes specific terms from the results.

For instance, a search for "OSINT AND "social media" NOT "cybersecurity"" would retrieve results related to OSINT and social media but exclude those related to cybersecurity.

Proximity operators, such as "NEAR" and "AROUND," allow OSINT practitioners to search for keywords or phrases that appear in close proximity to each other within a document or web page. These operators help identify content where concepts are closely related.

For example, "OSINT NEAR/3 "threat assessment"" would return results with "OSINT" and "threat assessment" appearing within three words of each other.

Wildcards, represented by asterisks (*) or question marks (?), can be used in search queries to replace unknown characters. The asterisk represents multiple characters, while the question mark represents a single character. Wildcards are helpful for finding variations of keywords or when specific spellings are uncertain.

A search for "cybersecurit* best practices" would retrieve results containing variations like "cybersecurity" and "cybersecuritization."

Parentheses can be used to group search terms and control the order of operations in complex queries. This allows OSINT practitioners to create intricate search strings with precision.

For example, "(OSINT OR "open-source intelligence") AND (tools OR techniques)" would help narrow down results to content related to either OSINT or open-source intelligence, along with either tools or techniques.

Search engines and databases often offer date range operators that enable users to filter results based on publication or modification dates. OSINT practitioners can use these operators to focus on recent or historical information, depending on their needs.

By specifying a date range like "before:2022-01-01" or "after:2022-01-01," practitioners can refine their searches to target information within specific time frames.

The "define" operator can be used to access quick definitions and explanations of terms. By using "define:" followed by a word or phrase, users can obtain concise definitions from various sources.

For example, "define:phishing" would provide definitions and explanations of the term "phishing" from reputable sources.

Geo-specific operators, such as "near," "location," or "around," allow OSINT practitioners to search for information related to a specific geographic area. These operators are valuable for narrowing down results to a particular location or region.

For instance, "cybersecurity near:New York City" would retrieve cybersecurity-related information specific to the New York City area.

The "cache" operator can be used to access cached versions of web pages that may no longer be available on the live internet. By using "cache:" followed by a web address, users can view the cached version of a page as it appeared when it was last crawled by search engines.

OSINT practitioners can take advantage of the "info" operator to access information about a specific website. By using "info:" followed by a web address, users can obtain details about the site, including links to cached pages, similar sites, and related searches.

In summary, exploring advanced search operators is a fundamental skill for OSINT practitioners, enabling them to conduct precise and targeted searches across the vast landscape of open-source information. These operators provide powerful tools for refining queries, specifying sources, filtering results, and uncovering relevant information. By mastering these operators, OSINT practitioners can enhance their ability to gather accurate and timely intelligence from online sources.

In the realm of open-source intelligence (OSINT), the ability to craft complex queries is a skill that empowers practitioners to dig deeper, uncover hidden information, and retrieve precise results from the vast expanse of online sources. Crafting complex OSINT queries involves combining advanced search operators, keywords, and logical structures to formulate queries that yield actionable intelligence.

The first step in crafting complex OSINT queries is to define the specific objectives and goals of the investigation or intelligence-gathering task. Having a clear understanding of what information is sought and why it is essential sets the foundation for constructing effective queries.

Next, OSINT practitioners must identify the key elements and variables relevant to their query. This includes determining the scope of the search, such as the time frame, geographic region, and specific sources to target. Identifying the most relevant keywords and phrases is crucial for constructing precise queries.

One of the fundamental principles of crafting complex OSINT queries is the use of advanced search operators. These operators, as explored in a previous chapter, enable practitioners to refine their searches and control the inclusion or exclusion of specific terms and criteria. Operators like "AND," "OR," "NOT," and "NEAR" provide powerful tools for combining keywords and logical conditions.

Boolean logic plays a central role in constructing complex queries. OSINT practitioners can use Boolean operators to create logical relationships between keywords and phrases. "AND" requires all terms to be present, "OR" broadens the search by including any of the terms, and "NOT" excludes specific terms from the results. Combining these operators allows practitioners to construct intricate queries that precisely filter information.

Parentheses are essential for controlling the order of operations in complex queries. By grouping keywords and operators within parentheses, practitioners can ensure that certain conditions are evaluated together. This allows for the creation of complex logical structures within a single query.

For example, consider the query: "(cybersecurity OR "information security") AND ("best practices" OR "risk management") NOT ("data breach" OR "incident report"). This query employs parentheses to group related terms and control logical relationships, resulting in a focused search for cybersecurity best practices and risk management while excluding results related to data breaches or incident reports.

Wildcard characters, such as asterisks (*) and question marks (?), can be incorporated into complex queries to account for variations in spelling or to search for unknown characters within keywords. Wildcards are particularly useful when dealing with terms that have multiple forms or when specific spellings are uncertain.

The "filetype" operator is an integral part of crafting complex OSINT queries when seeking specific types of documents or files. By using "filetype:" followed by an extension, practitioners can target results that match the desired file type. This is valuable for retrieving documents, spreadsheets, presentations, and other file formats relevant to the investigation.

Advanced search queries can also include date range operators to filter results based on publication or modification dates. OSINT practitioners can specify a date range to focus on recent or historical information, aligning with the investigation's time frame.

Crafting complex OSINT queries often involves geolocation operators to narrow down results to a specific geographic area or region of interest. These operators, such as "near," "location," or "around," are vital for targeting information relevant to a particular location.

Additionally, practitioners can incorporate domain-specific operators like "site" to restrict results to a specific website or domain. This is valuable when investigating a particular organization or source, ensuring that results are sourced exclusively from the designated site.

Using the "related" operator, OSINT practitioners can identify websites that are related to a specified URL. This operator expands the scope of research by uncovering websites with similar content or themes, providing a broader context for the investigation.

In crafting complex OSINT queries, practitioners should consider the ethical and legal implications of their searches. Respecting privacy, adhering to data protection regulations, and complying with platform policies are essential aspects of responsible OSINT query construction. Gathering information in a manner that respects individual rights and legal constraints is paramount.

Complex OSINT queries often require iterative refinement and testing. Practitioners may need to experiment with different combinations of keywords, operators, and logical structures to achieve the desired results. Regularly reviewing and adjusting queries based on the evolving nature of the investigation or intelligence task is crucial for success.

Collaboration among OSINT practitioners can be highly beneficial when crafting complex queries. Sharing insights, query templates, and best practices within the OSINT community fosters knowledge exchange and enables practitioners to leverage each other's expertise.

In summary, crafting complex OSINT queries is a skill that empowers practitioners to conduct targeted and precise investigations, extracting valuable intelligence from a vast array of online sources. By mastering advanced search operators, Boolean logic, and query construction techniques, OSINT practitioners can tailor their queries to meet specific objectives and uncover actionable information. Responsible query construction that respects ethical and legal considerations is essential, and iterative refinement and collaboration within the OSINT community enhance the effectiveness of complex OSINT queries.

Chapter 10: Legal and Ethical Considerations in OSINT

Navigating the legal landscape of open-source intelligence (OSINT) is an essential aspect of conducting responsible and ethical intelligence gathering in today's digital age. OSINT practitioners must be aware of the legal considerations, restrictions, and guidelines that govern the collection, analysis, and dissemination of information obtained from open sources.

The legal framework for OSINT can vary significantly from one jurisdiction to another, as it is influenced by national and international laws, regulations, and case precedents. Therefore, it is crucial for OSINT practitioners to understand the legal context within which they operate.

One fundamental legal principle that OSINT practitioners must adhere to is the respect for privacy rights. Privacy laws vary across countries and regions, but they generally protect individuals' rights to control their personal information and prevent its unauthorized collection or dissemination.

When conducting OSINT, practitioners should be cautious not to infringe upon individuals' privacy rights by avoiding the collection of sensitive personal data without proper consent or legal justification.

Additionally, copyright laws play a significant role in OSINT, particularly when it comes to using and sharing content obtained from the internet. Practitioners must respect copyright regulations and obtain appropriate permissions when using copyrighted materials.

Fair use and fair dealing exceptions may apply in some cases, allowing limited use of copyrighted materials for purposes such as criticism, comment, news reporting, or education.

However, the interpretation of fair use can vary, and it is essential to seek legal advice when unsure.

OSINT practitioners should also consider the terms of use and terms of service of online platforms and websites when collecting information. Many websites have specific policies that govern data scraping, automated data collection, and content sharing.

Violating these terms can result in legal consequences, such as legal action or being banned from using the platform. It is crucial to review and comply with platform-specific terms when conducting OSINT.

Publicly available information, often referred to as "publicly accessible" or "publicly disclosed" information, generally falls within the realm of open sources that OSINT practitioners can legally access and use. However, practitioners should be cautious when dealing with information that may have been inadvertently or unintentionally disclosed.

For example, while information posted on social media profiles with public settings is generally considered publicly accessible, practitioners should avoid exploiting security flaws or vulnerabilities to access non-public information.

Ethical considerations should guide OSINT practitioners' actions, even when they are within the bounds of the law. Respecting individuals' privacy, obtaining informed consent when necessary, and avoiding harmful or malicious activities are fundamental ethical principles.

OSINT practitioners should also be aware of international agreements and treaties that may impact their activities. For example, the General Data Protection Regulation (GDPR) in Europe has stringent rules regarding the collection and processing of personal data.

Practitioners who process personal data of European Union residents must comply with GDPR requirements, including obtaining explicit consent, providing data subjects with access to their information, and ensuring data security.

Additionally, OSINT practitioners should consider the ethical implications of their work, especially when dealing with sensitive or potentially harmful information. The potential consequences of OSINT activities should be carefully assessed, and steps should be taken to minimize harm and protect the well-being of individuals or organizations involved.

In some cases, OSINT practitioners may encounter legal restrictions related to national security and classified information. Handling, sharing, or disseminating information that is classified or protected by national security laws can result in severe legal consequences, including criminal charges.

Practitioners should exercise extreme caution when dealing with such information and ensure they are in compliance with national security regulations.

When OSINT practitioners gather information from online sources, they should always consider the reliability and credibility of the sources. Relying on unverified or unreliable sources can lead to inaccurate or misleading conclusions, which can have legal and reputational repercussions.

OSINT practitioners should take steps to verify the authenticity of the information they collect and be transparent about their sources and methods when presenting their findings.

Moreover, OSINT practitioners should be aware of the potential for misinformation and disinformation campaigns on the internet. The spread of false or misleading information can have significant societal and political implications.

Practitioners should exercise critical thinking and skepticism when encountering information that seems suspicious or lacks credible sources. They should also be cautious about unintentionally amplifying false information through their OSINT activities.

In summary, navigating the legal landscape of OSINT requires a deep understanding of privacy laws, copyright regulations, international agreements, and ethical principles. OSINT practitioners must always respect individuals' privacy rights, obtain proper consent, and comply with platform-specific terms of use.

They should also be aware of national security restrictions and exercise caution when handling sensitive or classified information. Additionally, verifying sources and being vigilant against misinformation and disinformation are crucial aspects of responsible OSINT practice.

By adhering to legal and ethical standards, OSINT practitioners can conduct intelligence gathering activities that are both effective and responsible.

Ethical guidelines are the cornerstone of responsible open-source intelligence (OSINT) practice, ensuring that OSINT practitioners conduct their activities with integrity, respect, and professionalism.

Practitioners must always prioritize the principles of honesty, transparency, and respect for individuals' rights and privacy when engaging in OSINT activities.

One of the fundamental ethical principles for OSINT practitioners is respecting privacy rights. Privacy is a fundamental human right, and OSINT practitioners must be cautious not to infringe upon individuals' privacy when collecting or using information from open sources.

Obtaining informed consent is crucial when conducting OSINT activities that involve the collection of personal or sensitive data. Practitioners should seek explicit permission from individuals before gathering and using their information, especially when it involves private or sensitive matters.

In cases where explicit consent is not possible or feasible, OSINT practitioners should exercise discretion and avoid the collection of sensitive personal information whenever possible.

Transparency is another key ethical principle in OSINT practice. Practitioners should be transparent about their intentions, methods, and sources when conducting intelligence-gathering activities.

Providing clear and accurate information about the purpose of the OSINT research, the data sources used, and the potential implications of the findings is essential for building trust and credibility.

In situations where OSINT practitioners are conducting investigations or research on behalf of organizations or clients, they should ensure that those parties are aware of and in agreement with the ethical principles and guidelines that govern the research.

Maintaining the integrity and accuracy of OSINT findings is paramount. Practitioners should strive to present information truthfully and objectively, avoiding any form of bias, manipulation, or distortion.

It is crucial to rely on reputable and credible sources when collecting and citing information. Verification of the authenticity and reliability of sources is a key responsibility of OSINT practitioners.

When using OSINT data, practitioners should be aware of the potential for misinformation and disinformation on the internet. Misinformation refers to false or inaccurate information shared without malicious intent, while disinformation is deliberately fabricated information with the intent to deceive.

OSINT practitioners should exercise critical thinking skills and skepticism when encountering information that appears suspicious or lacks credible sources. They should refrain from spreading unverified information and should not contribute to the dissemination of false or misleading content.

Responsible OSINT practitioners are mindful of the potential consequences of their activities. They should assess the potential harm that could result from their findings and take steps to minimize any negative impact.

When dealing with sensitive or potentially harmful information, practitioners should consider the ethical implications and prioritize the well-being and safety of individuals and organizations involved.

Practitioners should also be cautious about engaging in activities that may be perceived as harassment, stalking, or invasive in nature. Conducting OSINT research should not involve activities that could cause harm or distress to individuals or organizations.

Respecting copyright and intellectual property rights is essential in OSINT practice. Practitioners should comply with copyright regulations and obtain appropriate permissions when using copyrighted materials.

Fair use and fair dealing exceptions may apply in some cases, but practitioners should seek legal advice when unsure about the use of copyrighted content.

Additionally, when conducting OSINT activities, practitioners should be aware of national and international laws and regulations that may apply to their research. These may include privacy laws, data protection regulations, and national security restrictions.

Compliance with legal requirements is a fundamental ethical obligation, and practitioners should seek legal counsel when their OSINT activities involve potentially sensitive legal issues.

Collaboration and knowledge sharing within the OSINT community are encouraged, but practitioners should be respectful of each other's work and intellectual property. Proper attribution and acknowledgment of sources and contributions are ethical practices that foster a positive and supportive community.

Furthermore, ethical OSINT practitioners should continuously update their knowledge and skills to stay informed about evolving ethical considerations, legal requirements, and best practices in the field.

In summary, ethical guidelines for OSINT practitioners serve as a compass that guides their actions, ensuring that they conduct intelligence-gathering activities with integrity, transparency, and respect for privacy and ethical principles. Adhering to these guidelines not only safeguards the rights and well-being of individuals and organizations but also upholds the professionalism and credibility of the OSINT community. Responsible OSINT practice is not only about what practitioners can do but also about what they should do to ensure ethical and responsible intelligence gathering.

BOOK 2
MASTERING OSINT
ADVANCED TECHNIQUES WITH MITAKA

ROB BOTWRIGHT

Chapter 1: Exploring the Power of Mitaka

Harnessing the potential of Mitaka is a journey into the world of open-source intelligence (OSINT) automation and integration, where the power of this versatile tool can transform your investigative capabilities.

Mitaka is a Python framework that empowers OSINT practitioners to streamline and automate various intelligence-gathering tasks, enhancing efficiency and effectiveness.

At its core, Mitaka simplifies the process of interacting with OSINT data sources, allowing practitioners to access information from a wide range of platforms and services with ease.

With Mitaka, you can harness the collective intelligence of the internet by automating data collection, analysis, and reporting, all while maintaining the highest ethical and legal standards.

The versatility of Mitaka makes it suitable for a diverse range of OSINT applications, from threat intelligence and cybersecurity investigations to social media analysis and competitive research.

As you embark on your journey to harness the potential of Mitaka, it's essential to understand its key components and features.

Mitaka relies on a modular architecture, allowing users to integrate various OSINT tools, services, and data sources seamlessly. Each module is designed to interact with a specific OSINT resource, such as social media platforms, domain information, or threat intelligence feeds.

These modules can be customized and configured to meet your specific intelligence-gathering needs, ensuring that Mitaka adapts to your objectives and requirements.

Mitaka is highly extensible, and OSINT practitioners can develop their custom modules to interact with new data sources or enhance existing ones. This flexibility enables you to keep up with evolving OSINT challenges and stay ahead in the ever-changing landscape of online information.

In the world of OSINT, data visualization plays a crucial role in making sense of vast amounts of information. Mitaka excels in this regard, offering advanced data visualization capabilities that help you interpret and present OSINT findings effectively.

Whether you need to create timelines, charts, graphs, or other visual representations of your OSINT data, Mitaka provides the tools to transform raw information into actionable intelligence.

Mitaka's integration with mapping services enables geospatial analysis, allowing you to explore the geographical aspects of your OSINT investigations.

Geolocation and mapping capabilities can be invaluable for tracking the movements of individuals or understanding the geographical context of online activities.

When harnessing the potential of Mitaka, you'll discover its ability to automate repetitive and time-consuming OSINT tasks. By defining workflows and automation rules, you can streamline data collection, analysis, and reporting, saving valuable time and resources.

This automation not only boosts efficiency but also reduces the risk of errors that can occur in manual intelligence-gathering processes.

One of Mitaka's standout features is its integration with various OSINT tools and services, creating a cohesive and comprehensive OSINT ecosystem.

This integration enables you to leverage the capabilities of multiple tools simultaneously, expanding your investigative reach and enhancing your ability to gather critical intelligence.

Mitaka's built-in threat intelligence capabilities make it an indispensable tool for cybersecurity professionals and threat analysts. By integrating with threat intelligence feeds and sources, Mitaka can help you stay informed about emerging threats and vulnerabilities.

It allows you to monitor threat indicators, assess their relevance to your organization, and take proactive measures to mitigate risks.

Mitaka's support for data enrichment and correlation enhances your ability to connect the dots in complex OSINT investigations. You can cross-reference information from multiple sources, identifying relationships and uncovering hidden insights.

Mitaka's data enrichment capabilities can augment your intelligence with additional context, making your findings more robust and actionable.

Collaboration is a critical aspect of OSINT practice, and Mitaka facilitates teamwork by enabling multiple users to work on the same OSINT project simultaneously.

This collaborative approach fosters knowledge sharing, enables peer review of findings, and enhances the overall quality of intelligence gathered.

As you delve deeper into harnessing the potential of Mitaka, you'll find that its customization options allow you to tailor the tool to your unique requirements.

You can define your OSINT objectives, select the most relevant modules, and configure settings to align with your specific investigative needs.

Mitaka's adaptability extends to the integration of your custom scripts and tools, ensuring that you can seamlessly incorporate your existing OSINT resources into the Mitaka framework.

The ability to execute custom scripts within Mitaka workflows enhances your analytical capabilities and empowers you to address specialized OSINT challenges.

In your journey with Mitaka, you'll discover that it can serve as a force multiplier for your OSINT efforts. It enables you to achieve more in less time, freeing you to focus on the critical aspects of analysis and interpretation.

Mitaka's role in open-source intelligence goes beyond data collection; it empowers you to transform raw information into actionable insights that inform decision-making and support various objectives.

Mitaka's role in open-source intelligence goes beyond data collection; it empowers you to transform raw information into actionable insights that inform decision-making and support various objectives.

Furthermore, Mitaka's support for report generation simplifies the communication of OSINT findings. You can create detailed reports that encapsulate your intelligence-gathering process, findings, and recommendations, facilitating collaboration and knowledge sharing within your organization.

In your journey to harness the potential of Mitaka, you'll find that its user-friendly interface and intuitive controls make it accessible to OSINT practitioners with varying levels of technical expertise.

Whether you're a seasoned OSINT professional or a novice, Mitaka's user-centric design ensures that you can leverage its capabilities effectively.

Mitaka is continuously evolving, with updates and enhancements regularly released by its developer community. Staying up-to-date with these developments is essential to maximize the potential of Mitaka and adapt to emerging OSINT challenges.

In summary, harnessing the potential of Mitaka is a journey that empowers OSINT practitioners to streamline their intelligence-gathering processes, automate repetitive tasks, and enhance their analytical capabilities.

Mitaka's versatility, customization options, and integration with various OSINT tools and services make it a valuable asset for professionals across diverse domains, from cybersecurity and threat analysis to competitive intelligence and social media investigations.

By embracing Mitaka as a powerful OSINT tool, practitioners can navigate the complex landscape of open-source intelligence with confidence and efficiency, ultimately delivering more informed and impactful results.

Mitaka plays a pivotal role in the realm of open-source intelligence (OSINT) investigations, serving as a versatile and indispensable tool for OSINT practitioners across various domains and industries.

Its significance lies in its ability to streamline and automate crucial OSINT tasks, enabling practitioners to gather, analyze, and visualize data from a wide range of online sources efficiently and effectively.

One of Mitaka's primary roles in OSINT investigations is to act as a force multiplier, allowing practitioners to achieve more in less time. By automating repetitive data collection processes and providing a unified platform for interacting with diverse OSINT sources, Mitaka enhances productivity and accelerates the intelligence-gathering process.

Moreover, Mitaka simplifies the complex task of managing multiple OSINT tools and services by offering a modular and extensible framework. OSINT practitioners can seamlessly integrate various modules that cater to their specific investigative needs, creating a customized OSINT ecosystem tailored to their objectives.

Mitaka's modular architecture allows practitioners to choose from a wide array of pre-built modules, each designed to interact with different OSINT resources such as social media platforms, domain information databases, and threat intelligence feeds.

These modules can be configured, extended, or replaced as needed, ensuring that Mitaka adapts to the evolving requirements of each OSINT investigation.

Additionally, Mitaka fosters collaboration among OSINT practitioners, as it supports multiple users working on the same OSINT project simultaneously. This collaborative approach enhances knowledge sharing, enables peer review of findings, and promotes a collective effort in intelligence gathering.

Mitaka's role in OSINT investigations extends to data visualization, a critical aspect of making sense of vast amounts of information. Through advanced data visualization capabilities, Mitaka empowers practitioners to interpret and present OSINT findings effectively.

Whether creating timelines, charts, graphs, or other visual representations, Mitaka transforms raw data into actionable intelligence that is easy to understand and communicate.

Furthermore, Mitaka's geospatial analysis capabilities, achieved through integration with mapping services, enable practitioners to explore the geographical aspects of their OSINT investigations. This capability is invaluable for tracking the movements of individuals or understanding the geographical context of online activities.

Mitaka also excels in the realm of data enrichment and correlation, where practitioners can cross-reference information from multiple sources, identify relationships, and uncover hidden insights. By augmenting OSINT data with additional context, Mitaka enhances the robustness and depth of intelligence gathered.

The automation features of Mitaka go beyond data collection and extend to the execution of custom scripts and tools within OSINT workflows. This flexibility allows practitioners to address specialized OSINT challenges by seamlessly incorporating their existing resources into the Mitaka framework.

Mitaka's role in OSINT investigations is particularly pronounced in the field of cybersecurity and threat intelligence. It integrates with threat intelligence feeds and sources, enabling practitioners to monitor threat indicators, assess their relevance, and take proactive measures to mitigate risks.

Moreover, Mitaka's integration with mapping services enhances geospatial threat analysis, helping organizations identify and respond to threats with geographical components effectively.

Mitaka's advanced capabilities in OSINT investigations culminate in the generation of comprehensive reports. OSINT practitioners can use Mitaka to create detailed reports that encapsulate their intelligence-gathering process, findings, and recommendations.

These reports facilitate collaboration and knowledge sharing within organizations, enabling stakeholders to make informed decisions based on the intelligence provided.

Mitaka's user-friendly interface and intuitive controls make it accessible to OSINT practitioners with varying levels of technical expertise. Whether you are a seasoned OSINT professional or a novice, Mitaka's user-centric design ensures that you can leverage its capabilities effectively.

Additionally, Mitaka is continually evolving, with updates and enhancements released by its developer community. Staying current with these developments is essential to maximizing the potential of Mitaka and adapting to emerging OSINT challenges.

In summary, Mitaka's role in OSINT investigations is pivotal, as it empowers practitioners to streamline data collection, analysis, and visualization while promoting collaboration and automation. Mitaka's versatility and adaptability make it a valuable asset in diverse domains, from cybersecurity and threat analysis to competitive intelligence and social media investigations.

By embracing Mitaka as an essential OSINT tool, practitioners can navigate the complexities of open-source intelligence with confidence and efficiency, ultimately delivering more informed and impactful results.

Chapter 2: Customizing Mitaka for Your OSINT Needs

Adapting Mitaka to your workflow is a process that empowers open-source intelligence (OSINT) practitioners to customize this versatile tool to their specific needs and objectives.

Mitaka's flexibility and extensibility make it well-suited for integration into diverse OSINT workflows, allowing practitioners to streamline intelligence-gathering tasks and achieve greater efficiency.

The first step in adapting Mitaka to your workflow is to define your OSINT objectives and requirements clearly.

Consider the nature of your investigations, the types of data you need to collect, and the specific sources you intend to utilize. This initial planning stage is essential for tailoring Mitaka to meet your unique investigative needs.

Once you have a clear understanding of your objectives, explore Mitaka's modular architecture, which allows you to select and configure modules that align with your OSINT goals.

Mitaka offers a wide range of pre-built modules designed to interact with various OSINT resources, including social media platforms, domain information databases, and threat intelligence feeds.

Browse the available modules and choose those that best match your intended data sources and investigative requirements.

Customization is a key aspect of adapting Mitaka to your workflow.

While Mitaka provides a selection of pre-built modules, it also allows you to develop your custom modules to interact with new data sources or enhance existing ones.

Creating custom modules requires knowledge of Python programming, but it provides the opportunity to fine-tune Mitaka to your specific needs and access specialized OSINT resources.

When configuring Mitaka for your workflow, pay attention to the settings and parameters of the selected modules.

Adjust these settings to align with your data collection and analysis requirements, ensuring that Mitaka operates in a manner that optimally supports your objectives.

Mitaka's adaptability extends to the integration of your existing OSINT scripts and tools.

If you have proprietary or specialized tools that you use in your investigations, you can seamlessly incorporate them into the Mitaka framework, enhancing your analytical capabilities.

Mitaka's support for the execution of custom scripts within its workflows empowers you to address unique OSINT challenges effectively.

Consider how your OSINT investigations will benefit from automation.

Mitaka excels in automating repetitive data collection and analysis tasks, saving valuable time and reducing the risk of errors that can occur in manual processes.

By defining workflows and automation rules within Mitaka, you can create a streamlined intelligence-gathering process that aligns with your specific investigative needs.

As you adapt Mitaka to your workflow, keep in mind the importance of data visualization.

Mitaka offers advanced data visualization capabilities that enable you to transform raw information into actionable intelligence.

Whether you need to create timelines, charts, graphs, or other visual representations of your OSINT data, Mitaka provides the tools to present your findings effectively.

Consider the geographical aspects of your OSINT investigations.

Mitaka's integration with mapping services allows for geospatial analysis, which can be invaluable for tracking the movements of individuals or understanding the geographical context of online activities.

Configure Mitaka to leverage this capability if it aligns with your investigative objectives.

Mitaka's role in data enrichment and correlation is another aspect to explore.

The ability to cross-reference information from multiple sources can enhance the depth and reliability of your OSINT findings.

By connecting the dots and providing additional context, Mitaka strengthens the overall quality of your intelligence.

Collaboration is a fundamental aspect of OSINT practice, and Mitaka facilitates teamwork by supporting multiple users working on the same OSINT project simultaneously.

This collaborative approach fosters knowledge sharing, enables peer review of findings, and promotes a collective effort in intelligence gathering.

Mitaka's user-friendly interface and intuitive controls make it accessible to OSINT practitioners with varying levels of technical expertise.

Whether you are a seasoned OSINT professional or a novice, Mitaka's design ensures that you can leverage its capabilities effectively.

Stay informed about Mitaka's updates and enhancements, as the tool is continuously evolving.

Regularly check for new modules, features, and improvements released by the developer community to keep Mitaka aligned with emerging OSINT challenges and best practices.

In summary, adapting Mitaka to your workflow is a dynamic and customizable process that empowers OSINT practitioners to harness the full potential of this versatile tool.

Define your OSINT objectives clearly, select and configure modules that align with your data sources and requirements, and consider customization options to address unique challenges.

Utilize Mitaka's automation capabilities, data visualization tools, and geospatial analysis features to enhance your intelligence-gathering process.

Collaborate effectively with peers, and stay up-to-date with Mitaka's ongoing developments to ensure that your workflow remains optimized and aligned with the ever-evolving landscape of open-source intelligence.

Building custom Mitaka modules is a process that empowers open-source intelligence (OSINT) practitioners to extend the functionality of this powerful tool to meet their unique investigative needs.

Custom modules allow practitioners to interact with new OSINT data sources or enhance existing ones, providing flexibility and adaptability in intelligence gathering.

To embark on the journey of building custom Mitaka modules, you'll need a solid understanding of Python programming, as Mitaka is built on this language.

The first step in creating custom modules is to define the specific OSINT data source or service you want to interact with.

Consider the nature of the data, the type of information it provides, and how it aligns with your OSINT objectives.

Once you have a clear vision of your custom module's purpose, you can begin the development process.

Mitaka provides a comprehensive developer's guide that offers detailed instructions on creating custom modules.

Follow the guide carefully, as it will walk you through the necessary steps to create a module that seamlessly integrates with the Mitaka framework.

Custom modules are typically Python scripts that adhere to Mitaka's module structure and guidelines.

You'll need to import the required libraries and dependencies, define the module's functionality, and ensure that it can communicate effectively with Mitaka's core components.

The key to a successful custom module is thorough testing and validation.

Before deploying your module in a production OSINT environment, rigorously test it to ensure it functions as intended and interacts correctly with the data source.

Mitaka's modular architecture allows you to plug your custom module into the framework seamlessly.

You can configure Mitaka to recognize and use your module in conjunction with other pre-built modules to create a customized OSINT ecosystem tailored to your needs.

The ability to create custom modules provides OSINT practitioners with the flexibility to adapt to evolving data sources and investigative challenges.

Whether you need to access proprietary databases, specialized APIs, or unique online platforms, custom modules allow you to integrate these sources into your intelligence-gathering toolkit.

Furthermore, the extensibility of Mitaka ensures that your OSINT workflows remain up-to-date and aligned with emerging data sources and requirements.

Building custom Mitaka modules is not limited to data collection; you can also create modules for data analysis and visualization.

Custom modules can process and interpret data from various sources, providing you with deeper insights and facilitating the correlation of information.

This capability strengthens the overall quality and depth of your OSINT findings.

Additionally, custom modules can integrate advanced data visualization libraries, allowing you to create customized visual representations of your OSINT data.

These visualizations can enhance your ability to convey complex information effectively and support informed decision-making.

Consider the potential of your custom Mitaka module to automate data collection and analysis.

By defining automation rules and workflows within Mitaka, you can streamline intelligence-gathering tasks and save valuable time and resources.

Automation not only boosts efficiency but also reduces the risk of errors that can occur in manual processes.

The creation of custom modules extends beyond data collection and analysis to automation, allowing you to address unique OSINT challenges effectively.

When building custom modules, keep in mind that Mitaka's user-friendly interface and intuitive controls make it accessible to OSINT practitioners with varying levels of technical expertise.

Whether you are a seasoned developer or a novice, Mitaka's design ensures that you can leverage the capabilities of your custom modules effectively.

Collaboration is a fundamental aspect of OSINT practice, and custom modules can be shared within the Mitaka community.

This collaborative approach fosters knowledge sharing, enabling fellow practitioners to benefit from your custom modules and vice versa.

Sharing custom modules also contributes to the collective effort of intelligence gathering and supports the growth of the Mitaka ecosystem.

To ensure the long-term effectiveness of your custom Mitaka modules, stay informed about Mitaka's updates and enhancements.

Regularly check for new features, improvements, and community-contributed modules that align with your OSINT objectives and data sources.

By staying current with Mitaka's ongoing developments, you can maintain the relevance and adaptability of your custom modules in the ever-evolving landscape of open-source intelligence.

In summary, building custom Mitaka modules empowers OSINT practitioners to extend the capabilities of this versatile tool to meet their unique investigative needs.

Custom modules enable practitioners to interact with new data sources, enhance data analysis and visualization, and streamline intelligence-gathering processes.

By creating custom modules, OSINT practitioners can adapt to evolving data sources and requirements, ultimately enhancing the depth and quality of their OSINT findings.

Furthermore, sharing custom modules within the Mitaka community fosters collaboration and knowledge sharing, contributing to the growth of the Mitaka ecosystem and the collective effort in intelligence gathering.

Chapter 3: Leveraging Automation for OSINT Success

The automation advantage in open-source intelligence (OSINT) is a game-changer that revolutionizes the way intelligence practitioners gather and analyze information.

Automation streamlines and expedites data collection, analysis, and reporting, enhancing the efficiency and effectiveness of OSINT operations.

In an era where vast amounts of data are generated daily on the internet, automation provides the means to sift through this digital haystack and extract valuable needles of information.

One of the primary benefits of automation in OSINT is its ability to handle repetitive tasks with precision and consistency.

Tasks such as monitoring social media, tracking online mentions, or collecting data from numerous websites can be time-consuming and prone to human error when done manually.

Automation eliminates the need for manual intervention, ensuring that these tasks are carried out consistently and without fatigue.

Furthermore, automation allows OSINT practitioners to cover a broader scope of online sources and platforms.

It can simultaneously monitor multiple websites, forums, and social media networks, ensuring that no relevant information goes unnoticed.

This expanded coverage enhances the comprehensiveness of OSINT investigations and increases the chances of discovering critical insights.

Automation tools are adept at monitoring changes and updates on websites and online platforms.

They can detect modifications in web content, uncover new data, and notify practitioners promptly.

This real-time monitoring capability is invaluable for staying up-to-date with evolving situations and emerging threats.

Moreover, automation in OSINT supports the rapid processing of large datasets.

Tools can parse, categorize, and analyze vast amounts of unstructured data, transforming it into structured and actionable intelligence.

This capability enables OSINT practitioners to identify patterns, trends, and anomalies in data that would be challenging to discern manually.

Automation is not limited to data collection; it extends to data analysis as well.

Machine learning algorithms and natural language processing techniques can automate the analysis of text, sentiment, and linguistic patterns, providing valuable insights from textual data.

This automation enhances the speed and accuracy of information interpretation.

Furthermore, automation supports data enrichment and correlation.

Practitioners can automatically cross-reference information from various sources, connecting the dots and uncovering hidden relationships.

This integrated approach strengthens the reliability and relevance of OSINT findings.

Automation tools often come with advanced data visualization capabilities.

They can generate charts, graphs, and visual representations of OSINT data, making complex information more accessible and understandable.

These visualizations aid in conveying insights to decision-makers and stakeholders effectively.

Automation's role in OSINT extends to geospatial analysis.

It can extract geolocation data from online sources and plot it on maps, providing a geographical context to intelligence.

This capability is particularly valuable for tracking the movements of individuals or understanding the geographical distribution of online activities.

One of the significant advantages of automation is its ability to support alerting and notification systems.

Practitioners can set up automated alerts for specific keywords, events, or changes in data sources.

When triggered, these alerts notify practitioners in real-time, allowing them to respond promptly to emerging situations.

Moreover, automation enhances the consistency and repeatability of OSINT processes.

Once defined, automation workflows can be applied consistently to various OSINT investigations, reducing the likelihood of overlooking critical steps or making procedural errors.

This standardization ensures that OSINT operations adhere to best practices and organizational guidelines.

Automation can also contribute to threat intelligence and cybersecurity efforts.

It can monitor indicators of compromise (IoCs), assess their relevance, and provide early warnings of potential threats.

This proactive approach to threat detection helps organizations protect their assets and data from cyberattacks.

Furthermore, automation tools can aid in incident response by providing real-time data and analysis during security incidents.

Automation's efficiency extends to the reporting phase of OSINT investigations.

It can generate standardized reports that encapsulate the intelligence-gathering process, findings, and recommendations.

These reports are essential for communication and collaboration within organizations and with external stakeholders.

While automation brings numerous advantages to OSINT, it is not without challenges.

Practitioners must be cautious about the quality and accuracy of automated results.

Automation tools rely on algorithms and predefined rules, which may not always capture the nuances of context or intent.

Human oversight remains crucial to validate and interpret automated findings accurately.

Ethical considerations also come into play when using automation in OSINT.

Practitioners must ensure that automated data collection and analysis adhere to legal and ethical standards, respecting privacy and consent.

Moreover, the fast-paced nature of online information means that automation must be regularly updated and adjusted to remain effective.

New websites, platforms, and data sources continually emerge, requiring ongoing maintenance and adaptation of automation tools.

In summary, the automation advantage in OSINT represents a significant leap forward in intelligence gathering and analysis.

Automation streamlines data collection, analysis, and reporting, enhancing efficiency, coverage, and the comprehensiveness of OSINT investigations.

It supports real-time monitoring, large dataset processing, data enrichment, and data correlation, delivering valuable insights from vast amounts of digital information.

Automation tools aid in data visualization, geospatial analysis, and alerting, enabling practitioners to respond quickly to emerging situations and threats.

However, practitioners must exercise caution to ensure the quality and ethical use of automated results while staying vigilant about the evolving online landscape. Mitaka automation strategies are pivotal for open-source intelligence (OSINT) practitioners aiming to optimize their intelligence-gathering processes and enhance their analytical capabilities. Strategically implementing automation in Mitaka can significantly improve the efficiency, accuracy, and scalability of OSINT operations.

One of the fundamental Mitaka automation strategies is to identify and prioritize tasks that can benefit from automation. Begin by conducting a thorough analysis of your OSINT workflows to pinpoint repetitive, time-consuming, or data-intensive activities that are prime candidates for automation. For example, data collection from social media platforms, web scraping, or monitoring online mentions can be automated to save time and reduce manual effort.

Once you've identified suitable automation candidates, it's crucial to select the right automation tools and modules within Mitaka.

Mitaka offers a wide range of pre-built modules and integrations that can streamline various aspects of OSINT operations.

Choose modules that align with your specific automation needs and data sources, ensuring that they integrate seamlessly into your Mitaka workflow.

Customization is a key element of effective automation in Mitaka.

Consider developing custom automation scripts or modules tailored to your unique OSINT requirements.

This approach allows you to fine-tune automation processes, address specialized challenges, and extract maximum value from Mitaka's automation capabilities.

When designing automation workflows in Mitaka, establish clear objectives and define key performance indicators (KPIs) to measure the success of your automation strategies.

Clearly articulated goals help guide the development and implementation of automation processes, ensuring that they align with your OSINT objectives.

Automation in Mitaka extends to real-time monitoring and alerting.

Configure automated alerts based on specific triggers, such as keywords, events, or changes in data sources.

These alerts notify you promptly when relevant information surfaces, enabling swift responses to emerging situations or threats.

Another essential strategy is to embrace data enrichment and correlation through automation.

Mitaka can automatically cross-reference information from multiple sources, helping you identify relationships, patterns, and hidden insights in your OSINT data.

This integrated approach enhances the depth and quality of your intelligence.

Consider incorporating automation into your geospatial analysis efforts.

Mitaka can extract geolocation data from online sources and plot it on maps, providing valuable geographical context to your OSINT investigations.

This capability is especially valuable for tracking the movements of individuals or understanding the spatial distribution of online activities.

Workflow optimization is a key component of Mitaka automation strategies.

Streamline your automation processes by defining efficient workflows that minimize redundant tasks and maximize productivity.

Automation workflows should be well-documented and easily accessible to all team members involved in OSINT operations.

Mitaka's advanced data visualization capabilities can enhance your automation strategies.

Automate the generation of charts, graphs, and visual representations of your OSINT data to make complex information more accessible and comprehensible.

These visualizations aid in conveying insights effectively to decision-makers and stakeholders.

Mitaka's modular architecture allows for flexible and modular automation strategies.

You can build automation workflows that consist of a series of interconnected modules, each performing a specific task.

This modular approach enables you to create customized automation sequences that cater to your OSINT needs.

Continuous monitoring and adjustment are vital aspects of Mitaka automation strategies.

Regularly review the performance of your automation processes, and be prepared to adapt and refine them as needed.

The dynamic nature of the online landscape requires ongoing adjustments to automation tools and workflows to remain effective.

Collaboration is a fundamental component of Mitaka automation strategies.

Facilitate collaboration among OSINT practitioners by implementing automation processes that support multiple users working on the same OSINT project simultaneously.

This collaborative approach fosters knowledge sharing, peer review, and collective efforts in intelligence gathering.

When implementing Mitaka automation strategies, it's crucial to maintain a balance between automation and human oversight.

While automation enhances efficiency, human judgment and validation are essential to ensure the quality and accuracy of automated results.

Ethical considerations are paramount when employing automation in OSINT.

Ensure that your automation strategies comply with legal and ethical standards, respecting privacy, consent, and data protection regulations.

In summary, Mitaka automation strategies are instrumental in streamlining and enhancing OSINT operations.

Identify automation candidates, select the right tools and modules, and customize automation workflows to align with your OSINT objectives.

Establish clear goals, configure real-time monitoring and alerting, and embrace data enrichment and correlation.

Optimize workflows, leverage data visualization, and adapt automation processes to the dynamic online landscape.

Encourage collaboration and maintain a balance between automation and human oversight, all while adhering to ethical principles and legal standards.

By implementing effective Mitaka automation strategies, OSINT practitioners can unlock the full potential of automation to strengthen their intelligence-gathering capabilities.

Chapter 4: Targeted Data Collection with Mitaka

Precision data gathering with Mitaka represents a critical aspect of open-source intelligence (OSINT) operations that empowers practitioners to extract high-quality information with accuracy and relevance.

In an era where the internet is flooded with an overwhelming amount of data, the ability to pinpoint and collect precise data is essential for informed decision-making and threat detection.

The foundation of precision data gathering begins with a clear understanding of your OSINT objectives.

Before initiating data collection in Mitaka, define the specific information you seek, the sources where it can be found, and the context in which it will be utilized.

This clarity guides your data collection efforts, ensuring that you target the most relevant and valuable data.

Mitaka offers a versatile range of pre-built modules and integrations designed to interact with various online sources.

Select the modules that align with your data requirements, taking into account the sources, platforms, and websites where your target data is likely to reside.

Customization is a key element of precision data gathering.

Mitaka allows practitioners to create custom modules or scripts tailored to their unique data collection needs.

If the pre-built modules do not cover your specific requirements, consider developing custom modules that can extract data from specialized sources or websites.

Effective precision data gathering often involves setting up automated data collection processes.

Define automation workflows within Mitaka that continuously monitor and collect data from your chosen sources.

Automation not only saves time but also ensures that data is gathered consistently and promptly.

Consider using Mitaka's real-time monitoring and alerting capabilities to stay informed about updates and changes on the sources you are tracking.

Configuring alerts for specific keywords or events can notify you immediately when relevant data becomes available.

Precision data gathering extends to the effective use of advanced search operators.

Mitaka provides the ability to craft complex search queries that narrow down the scope of your data collection efforts.

Leverage Boolean operators, wildcards, and other search modifiers to refine your queries and extract data with pinpoint accuracy.

When conducting precision data gathering in Mitaka, it's essential to validate the data quality.

Data collected from online sources may vary in accuracy and reliability.

Implement data validation processes to assess the authenticity and credibility of the gathered information.

Cross-referencing data from multiple sources can enhance data quality and mitigate the risk of relying on inaccurate or biased information.

Incorporate data enrichment into your precision data gathering strategy.

Mitaka can automatically enrich data by adding additional context or details to the collected information.

For example, geolocation data, timestamps, or social media profiles can provide valuable context to OSINT findings.

Ensure that your precision data gathering efforts adhere to ethical and legal standards.

Respect privacy, obtain necessary permissions when applicable, and handle data in compliance with data protection regulations.

Ethical considerations are paramount in OSINT, and precision data gathering should be conducted with integrity and respect for individuals' rights.

Collaboration is a valuable asset in precision data gathering.

Mitaka supports multiple users working on the same OSINT project simultaneously, enabling knowledge sharing and peer review of collected data.

Collaborative efforts can enhance the accuracy and comprehensiveness of OSINT findings.

Regularly review and update your precision data gathering strategies to adapt to evolving data sources and requirements.

The online landscape is dynamic, with new sources and platforms emerging regularly.

Stay informed about changes in online sources, websites, and social media platforms to ensure that your data collection efforts remain effective.

Precision data gathering with Mitaka is an iterative process that requires continuous refinement and optimization.

In summary, precision data gathering with Mitaka is a crucial component of successful OSINT operations.

Start with a clear understanding of your objectives and target data, select the appropriate modules and sources, and consider customization when necessary.

Automation, real-time monitoring, and advanced search operators can enhance the accuracy and efficiency of data collection.

Validate data quality, incorporate data enrichment, and adhere to ethical and legal standards throughout the process.

Collaborate with peers and stay agile by adapting your precision data gathering strategies to the ever-evolving online landscape.

By following these principles, OSINT practitioners can master precision data gathering and leverage Mitaka's capabilities to extract valuable, accurate, and relevant information for their intelligence needs.

Extracting targeted insights from open-source intelligence (OSINT) data is a multifaceted process that requires a systematic approach and a keen analytical eye.

While the internet is a vast source of information, the challenge lies in sifting through the digital noise to uncover relevant and actionable insights.

To begin the process of extracting targeted insights, it's essential to define the scope and objectives of your OSINT investigation.

Clearly articulate what specific information or intelligence you seek, whether it's related to a person, organization, event, or topic.

This clarity will guide your efforts and help you focus on collecting data that directly contributes to your objectives.

When gathering data for targeted insights, start with reputable and authoritative sources.

These sources are more likely to provide accurate and trustworthy information, reducing the risk of relying on unreliable or misleading data.

Mitaka offers a range of pre-built modules and integrations that can help you access data from well-established online platforms, social media networks, news outlets, and more.

Customization plays a crucial role in the extraction of targeted insights.

Consider developing custom Mitaka modules or scripts tailored to your specific data requirements.

Custom modules enable you to interact with specialized data sources or websites that may not be covered by pre-built modules.

Moreover, custom modules allow you to fine-tune data collection to meet your unique needs.

Automation is a valuable asset in the extraction of targeted insights.

Configure Mitaka to automate data collection processes, ensuring that relevant data is continuously monitored and collected.

Automated workflows can save time and resources, especially when collecting data from sources that frequently update or change.

Mitaka's real-time monitoring and alerting capabilities complement the automation process.

Set up alerts based on specific triggers, such as keywords or events, to receive notifications when relevant information surfaces.

These alerts allow you to respond promptly to emerging situations or critical developments.

Precision is key when extracting targeted insights.

Leverage Mitaka's advanced search operators to craft specific and focused queries that narrow down the scope of data collection.

Boolean operators, wildcards, and search modifiers can help you refine your queries and extract data with pinpoint accuracy.

Cross-referencing and data correlation are powerful techniques for extracting insights.

Combine data from multiple sources to validate and enrich your findings.

Cross-referencing data enhances data quality and reduces the risk of relying on single-source information.

Data enrichment, such as adding geolocation data or timestamps to your findings, provides valuable context and depth to your insights.

Data validation is a critical step in the extraction process.

Verify the authenticity and credibility of the collected information.

Check the reliability of your sources and assess the consistency of the data.

Data validation helps ensure that the insights you extract are accurate and trustworthy.

Ethical considerations are paramount in OSINT, and they should guide your actions throughout the process of extracting targeted insights.

Respect privacy, obtain necessary permissions when applicable, and handle data in compliance with data protection regulations.

Incorporate ethical principles into your OSINT practices to maintain integrity and respect for individuals' rights.

Collaboration is a valuable resource when extracting targeted insights.

Mitaka supports multiple users working on the same OSINT project simultaneously, fostering knowledge sharing and peer review.

Collaboration enhances the quality and comprehensiveness of the insights you extract, as it allows for diverse perspectives and expertise.

Regularly review and update your data collection strategies to adapt to evolving data sources and requirements.

The online landscape is dynamic, with new platforms, websites, and data sources emerging continuously.

Staying informed about these changes ensures that your data collection efforts remain effective.

Extracting targeted insights is an iterative process that demands continuous refinement and optimization.

In summary, extracting targeted insights from OSINT data is a systematic and focused process that requires clear objectives, reliable sources, customization, automation, and precision.

Mitaka offers a range of tools and capabilities to aid in this process, from advanced search operators to real-time monitoring and data validation.

Ethical considerations should guide every step of the process to ensure integrity and respect for privacy.

Collaboration and adaptation are key elements in extracting high-quality insights from a dynamic online landscape.

By following these principles and leveraging Mitaka's capabilities, OSINT practitioners can extract targeted insights that contribute to informed decision-making and intelligence analysis.

Chapter 5: Mitaka and Social Media Intelligence

Enhancing social media investigations with Mitaka is a strategic approach that empowers open-source intelligence (OSINT) practitioners to leverage the vast and dynamic landscape of social media platforms effectively.

Social media platforms have become a prolific source of information, with millions of users sharing their thoughts, activities, and interactions online.

For OSINT practitioners, these platforms present a wealth of data that can be invaluable for investigations, threat assessments, and intelligence gathering.

However, the sheer volume of information on social media makes it challenging to extract relevant insights efficiently.

Mitaka offers a comprehensive toolkit that can enhance the entire process of social media investigations, from data collection and analysis to real-time monitoring and alerting.

To enhance social media investigations with Mitaka, it's essential to begin with a clear understanding of your objectives and target data.

Define the specific information you are seeking on social media platforms, whether it's related to individuals, organizations, events, or trends.

This clarity will guide your efforts and help you focus on collecting and analyzing data that directly contributes to your investigation.

Mitaka provides pre-built modules and integrations designed to interact with various social media platforms.

Select the modules that align with your social media investigation goals and the platforms where your target data is likely to reside.

These modules are tailored to extract data from popular social media networks, such as Twitter, Facebook, Instagram, and LinkedIn.

Customization is a key element in enhancing social media investigations.

Mitaka allows practitioners to create custom modules or scripts to meet specific data collection requirements.

Custom modules enable you to access data from specialized sources or platforms that may not be covered by pre-built modules.

Moreover, customization allows you to fine-tune data collection processes to meet the unique needs of your investigation.

Automation plays a crucial role in enhancing social media investigations.

Configure Mitaka to automate data collection processes on social media platforms, ensuring that relevant data is continuously monitored and gathered.

Automation saves time and resources, especially when dealing with high-volume data streams from social media.

Mitaka's real-time monitoring and alerting capabilities complement the automation process.

Set up alerts based on specific triggers, such as keywords, hashtags, or user mentions, to receive notifications when relevant information surfaces on social media.

These alerts enable you to stay updated on emerging developments and respond promptly to critical events.

Precision is a fundamental aspect of enhancing social media investigations.

Leverage Mitaka's advanced search operators to craft precise queries that narrow down the scope of data collection on social media.

Boolean operators, wildcards, and search modifiers can help you refine your queries and extract data with pinpoint accuracy. Cross-referencing and data correlation are powerful techniques in social media investigations.

Combine data from multiple social media platforms to validate and enrich your findings.

Cross-referencing data enhances the reliability of your insights and reduces the risk of relying on single-source information.

Data enrichment, such as adding geolocation data or timestamps to your findings, provides valuable context and depth to your social media investigation results.

Data validation is a critical step in enhancing social media investigations.Verify the authenticity and credibility of the collected information from social media sources.

Check the reliability of the sources themselves and assess the consistency of the data.

Data validation ensures that the insights you extract from social media are accurate and trustworthy.

Ethical considerations are paramount in OSINT, especially when conducting social media investigations.

Respect privacy, obtain necessary permissions when applicable, and handle data in compliance with data protection regulations.

Incorporate ethical principles into your social media investigation practices to maintain integrity and respect for individuals' rights.

Collaboration is a valuable asset in enhancing social media investigations.

Mitaka supports multiple users working on the same OSINT project simultaneously, fostering knowledge sharing and peer review of collected social media data.

Collaborative efforts can enhance the quality and comprehensiveness of the insights you extract from social media platforms.

Regularly review and update your social media investigation strategies to adapt to evolving platforms and trends.

The landscape of social media is dynamic, with new platforms, features, and communication patterns emerging regularly.

Staying informed about these changes ensures that your social media investigation efforts remain effective.

Enhancing social media investigations with Mitaka is an iterative process that demands continuous refinement and optimization.

In summary, enhancing social media investigations with Mitaka is a strategic approach that involves clear objectives, customization, automation, precision, data validation, and ethical considerations.

Mitaka's comprehensive toolkit and capabilities offer valuable resources for OSINT practitioners seeking to harness the wealth of data on social media platforms.

Collaboration and adaptation are essential elements in enhancing social media investigations, ensuring that insights are accurate and relevant in a dynamic online landscape.

By following these principles and leveraging Mitaka's capabilities, OSINT practitioners can enhance their social media investigation efforts and extract valuable intelligence from the world of social media. Mitaka offers a wide array of techniques and capabilities specifically designed to harness the power of social media data for open-source intelligence (OSINT) practitioners. These techniques are invaluable in extracting valuable insights, tracking trends, and monitoring events across various social media platforms.

To effectively leverage Mitaka techniques for social media data, it is crucial to begin with a clear understanding of your OSINT objectives and the specific information you aim to extract from social media.

Whether you are investigating individuals, organizations, or trends, defining your goals is essential in guiding your data collection and analysis efforts.

Mitaka provides pre-built modules and integrations tailored to interact with popular social media platforms, such as Twitter, Facebook, Instagram, and LinkedIn.

Select the modules that align with your social media data needs and the platforms where your target data resides.

These pre-built modules offer a streamlined approach to accessing and extracting data from various social media networks.

Customization plays a pivotal role in maximizing the effectiveness of Mitaka techniques for social media data.

Consider developing custom modules or scripts to meet specific data collection requirements that may not be covered by pre-built modules.

Customization allows you to fine-tune your data collection processes to cater to the unique needs of your OSINT investigation.

Automation is a fundamental technique when dealing with social media data.

Mitaka allows you to configure automated workflows that continuously monitor and collect data from social media platforms.

Automation not only saves time but also ensures that relevant data is consistently gathered.

Mitaka's real-time monitoring and alerting capabilities complement the automation process.

Set up alerts based on specific triggers, such as keywords, hashtags, or user mentions, to receive timely notifications when relevant information surfaces on social media.

These alerts enable you to stay updated on emerging developments and respond promptly to critical events.

Precision is paramount when employing Mitaka techniques for social media data.

Leverage advanced search operators, such as Boolean operators, wildcards, and search modifiers, to craft precise queries that narrow down the scope of your data collection efforts.

These operators help you refine your queries and extract data with pinpoint accuracy.

Cross-referencing and data correlation are powerful techniques to enhance the quality of social media data.

Combine data from multiple social media platforms to validate and enrich your findings.

Cross-referencing data enhances data reliability and reduces the risk of relying on single-source information.

Data enrichment, such as adding geolocation data or timestamps to your findings, provides valuable context and depth to your social media data analysis.

Data validation is a crucial step in Mitaka techniques for social media data.

Verify the authenticity and credibility of the collected information from social media sources.

Assess the reliability of the sources themselves and ensure the consistency of the data.

Data validation safeguards the accuracy and trustworthiness of the insights derived from social media.

Mitaka's capabilities are rooted in ethical considerations, especially when dealing with social media data.

Respect privacy, obtain necessary permissions when applicable, and handle data in compliance with data protection regulations.

Mitigate ethical concerns by incorporating principles of integrity and respect for individuals' rights into your OSINT practices.

Collaboration is an asset in harnessing Mitaka techniques for social media data.

Mitaka supports multiple users working on the same OSINT project simultaneously, fostering knowledge sharing and peer review of collected social media data.

Collaborative efforts enhance the quality and comprehensiveness of the insights you extract from social media platforms.

Regularly review and update your strategies for Mitaka techniques in social media data to adapt to the evolving landscape of social media platforms and trends.

Stay informed about changes in online behavior, communication patterns, and the emergence of new platforms to ensure the effectiveness of your social media data collection efforts.

Mitaka techniques for social media data are iterative processes that require continuous refinement and optimization.

In summary, Mitaka offers a diverse range of techniques and capabilities for extracting valuable insights from social media data in open-source intelligence (OSINT) operations.

Clear objectives, customization, automation, precision, data validation, and ethical considerations are fundamental principles in effectively leveraging these techniques.

Collaboration and adaptability are essential elements to ensure that insights drawn from social media data are accurate and relevant in the dynamic online landscape.

By following these principles and harnessing Mitaka's capabilities, OSINT practitioners can unlock the full potential of social media data for intelligence and investigative purposes.

Chapter 6: Advanced Analysis and Visualization

Advanced data analysis with Mitaka represents a crucial phase in the open-source intelligence (OSINT) process, where practitioners transform raw information into actionable intelligence.

While data collection is a significant part of OSINT, the true value lies in the ability to analyze and extract meaningful insights from the gathered data.

Mitaka offers an array of advanced data analysis techniques and tools that enable OSINT practitioners to uncover hidden patterns, trends, and connections within their datasets.

To effectively engage in advanced data analysis with Mitaka, it's imperative to start with a clear understanding of your OSINT objectives and the specific insights you aim to derive from your data.

Define the scope of your analysis, whether it pertains to individuals, organizations, events, or topics, to guide your analytical efforts.

Mitaka provides pre-built modules and integrations that facilitate data analysis across various domains, including social media, websites, and online forums.

Select the modules that align with your analytical needs and the sources where your data is derived.

These pre-built modules streamline the process of importing, organizing, and processing data for analysis.

Customization plays a pivotal role in advanced data analysis with Mitaka.

Consider developing custom modules or scripts tailored to your specific analytical requirements.

Custom modules allow you to implement specialized algorithms or techniques that may not be covered by pre-built modules, enhancing the depth and breadth of your analysis.

Automation is a fundamental component of advanced data analysis with Mitaka.

Configure automated workflows that facilitate the continuous processing and analysis of your data.

Automation not only increases efficiency but also ensures that your analysis remains up-to-date, particularly when dealing with dynamic data sources.

Mitaka's real-time monitoring and alerting capabilities complement the automation process.

Set up alerts based on specific triggers, such as changes in data patterns or the emergence of new information, to receive timely notifications and respond swiftly to critical developments.

Data cleansing and preprocessing are essential steps in advanced data analysis.

Mitaka offers tools for cleaning and transforming data, including removing duplicates, handling missing values, and normalizing data for consistent analysis.

Clean and well-preprocessed data sets the foundation for meaningful analysis outcomes.

Advanced data analysis often involves statistical techniques to uncover patterns and trends within your data.

Mitaka provides integration with statistical software and libraries, enabling you to perform various statistical analyses, such as regression analysis, hypothesis testing, and clustering.

These techniques help you identify relationships and dependencies within your data.

Machine learning and artificial intelligence (AI) are powerful tools in advanced data analysis with Mitaka.

Leverage machine learning algorithms to predict outcomes, classify data, and detect anomalies within your datasets.

AI-driven techniques can uncover intricate insights that may be challenging to discover through traditional analysis methods.

Visualization is a key aspect of advanced data analysis.

Mitaka offers visualization tools to create charts, graphs, and interactive dashboards that facilitate the exploration and presentation of your analysis results.

Visualizations provide a clear and concise way to communicate complex insights to stakeholders.

Incorporate geospatial analysis into your advanced data analysis when relevant.

Mitaka supports geospatial data visualization and analysis, allowing you to explore geographic patterns and relationships within your data.

This is particularly useful when dealing with location-based information.

Data fusion and integration are essential for holistic analysis.

Combine data from multiple sources, both within and outside Mitaka, to enrich your analysis and gain a comprehensive understanding of your subject.

Cross-referencing data enhances the reliability of your insights and reduces the risk of relying on single-source information.

Ethical considerations are paramount in advanced data analysis with Mitaka.

Respect privacy, adhere to data protection regulations, and handle sensitive information with care.

Ensure that your analysis practices align with ethical standards, and be mindful of the potential impact of your findings on individuals and organizations.

Collaboration is a valuable asset in advanced data analysis.

Mitaka supports multiple users working on the same OSINT project simultaneously, enabling knowledge sharing and peer review of analysis outcomes.

Collaborative efforts can enhance the quality and robustness of your analysis.

Regularly review and update your advanced data analysis strategies to adapt to evolving data sources and analytical requirements.

Stay informed about emerging analysis techniques, tools, and best practices to maintain the relevance and effectiveness of your analysis.

Advanced data analysis with Mitaka is an iterative process that demands continuous refinement and optimization.

In summary, advanced data analysis with Mitaka represents a critical phase in the OSINT process, where practitioners extract meaningful insights from gathered data.

Clear objectives, customization, automation, preprocessing, statistical analysis, machine learning, visualization, geospatial analysis, and ethical considerations are fundamental principles in conducting advanced data analysis.

Collaboration and adaptability are essential elements to ensure that analysis outcomes are accurate and actionable.

By following these principles and leveraging Mitaka's capabilities, OSINT practitioners can uncover valuable intelligence from their data, contributing to informed decision-making and threat detection. Visualizing OSINT findings with Mitaka is a critical step in transforming data into actionable insights that can inform decision-making and intelligence analysis.

Data, in its raw form, can be overwhelming and challenging to interpret effectively.

Visualizations serve as powerful tools to simplify complex information, highlight patterns, and communicate findings clearly to both technical and non-technical stakeholders.

To begin visualizing OSINT findings with Mitaka, it's essential to have a clear understanding of your objectives and the specific insights you intend to convey through visual representations.

Define the scope of your visualization, whether it pertains to individuals, organizations, events, or trends, to guide your efforts effectively.

Mitaka provides a range of visualization tools and capabilities that cater to various data types and analytical needs.

Select the visualization techniques that align with your objectives and the nature of your OSINT findings.

These tools enable you to create charts, graphs, maps, and interactive dashboards that enhance your ability to explore, interpret, and communicate data.

Customization plays a pivotal role in visualizing OSINT findings with Mitaka.

Tailor your visualizations to meet specific requirements, such as color schemes, labeling, and formatting, to ensure that they effectively convey the intended message.

Customization allows you to adapt visualizations to the preferences and needs of your audience.

Mitaka supports geospatial data visualization, making it a valuable asset when dealing with location-based OSINT findings.

Leverage geospatial visualization techniques to display data on maps, identify geographic patterns, and visualize the spatial distribution of information.

This is particularly useful when analyzing data related to events, incidents, or the movement of individuals or assets.

Visualization is not limited to static images; Mitaka enables the creation of dynamic and interactive visualizations.

Interactive dashboards empower users to explore data interactively, filter information, and drill down into specific details, enhancing their engagement with the findings.

These dashboards are effective in facilitating data-driven decision-making and fostering a deeper understanding of complex OSINT insights.

Ethical considerations are paramount in visualizing OSINT findings.

Respect privacy, adhere to data protection regulations, and handle sensitive information with care when preparing visualizations.

Ensure that your visualizations do not inadvertently disclose confidential or personally identifiable information.

Collaboration is a valuable asset in visualizing OSINT findings with Mitaka.

Multiple users can collaborate on the same OSINT project simultaneously, allowing for knowledge sharing and peer review of visualizations.

Collaboration enhances the quality and comprehensiveness of the insights you communicate through visual representations.

Regularly review and update your visualization strategies to adapt to evolving data sources, analytical requirements, and stakeholder needs.

Stay informed about emerging visualization techniques, tools, and best practices to maintain the relevance and effectiveness of your visualizations.

Incorporate storytelling into your visualizations to make the findings more compelling and memorable.

Narrative-driven visualizations guide the audience through the data, providing context and meaning to the information presented.

Tell a coherent and persuasive story that conveys the significance of the OSINT findings and their implications.

Mitaka's visualization capabilities extend to both static and dynamic visual representations.

Static visualizations include charts, graphs, and maps that capture a snapshot of the data at a specific point in time.

These visualizations are effective for presenting key insights and trends in a concise and straightforward manner.

Dynamic visualizations, on the other hand, offer an interactive experience that allows users to explore data in real time.

These visualizations are particularly valuable for scenarios where users need to interact with data, filter information, and gain deeper insights.

Select the appropriate type of visualization based on the nature of your OSINT findings and the intended audience.

Consider the visual literacy of your audience when designing visualizations.

Ensure that the visual representations are clear, intuitive, and easy to interpret, even for individuals who may not have extensive data analysis experience.

Mitaka offers a variety of chart types, such as bar charts, line graphs, pie charts, and scatter plots, to cater to diverse data visualization needs.

Choose the chart type that best suits your data and the insights you aim to convey.

For example, use bar charts to compare quantities, line graphs to track trends over time, and pie charts to represent proportions.

Utilize color effectively in your visualizations to highlight important information and create visual contrast.

However, be mindful of color choices, as excessive use of color can lead to confusion or misinterpretation.

Consider using color palettes that are accessible to individuals with color vision deficiencies.

Interactivity in dynamic visualizations can significantly enhance the user experience.

Enable users to interact with data points, zoom in on specific areas of interest, and apply filters to focus on particular aspects of the findings.

Interactive elements empower users to explore data independently and gain deeper insights.

Mitaka supports the integration of external data sources into visualizations.

This capability allows you to enrich OSINT findings with additional context or data from external databases, APIs, or sources.

External data integration can provide valuable background information and enhance the comprehensiveness of your visualizations.

Annotations and labels play a crucial role in clarifying visualizations.

Include descriptive labels, titles, and annotations to provide context and explain the significance of data points, trends, or patterns.

Annotations help users understand the key takeaways from the visual representation.

Effective data storytelling involves structuring your visualizations to guide the audience through a logical narrative.

Begin with an introduction that sets the context and outlines the purpose of the visualization.

Progressively reveal insights, highlight key findings, and conclude with a clear and compelling message.

Mitaka's capabilities support the creation of dynamic and interactive data storytelling experiences.

Stakeholder engagement is essential in visualizing OSINT findings.

Engage with stakeholders throughout the visualization process to understand their requirements, gather feedback, and tailor visualizations to their needs.

Effective communication and collaboration with stakeholders ensure that visualizations align with their goals and objectives.

Data security and confidentiality should always be a top priority when working with OSINT findings.

Protect sensitive information, and be mindful of data privacy regulations when sharing visualizations with stakeholders.

Ensure that visualizations do not inadvertently disclose confidential or personally identifiable information.

Accessibility is a critical consideration in visualizing OSINT findings.

Create visualizations that are accessible to individuals with disabilities, such as screen readers, by providing alternative text descriptions and ensuring compatibility with accessibility standards.

Mitaka's visualization capabilities include features that facilitate accessibility, such as text-to-speech support.

In summary, visualizing OSINT findings with Mitaka is a critical step in transforming raw data into actionable insights.

Clear objectives, customization, ethical considerations, collaboration, and storytelling are fundamental principles in creating effective visualizations.

Leverage Mitaka's versatile visualization tools and capabilities to communicate OSINT insights clearly, whether through static charts or interactive dashboards.

Stay updated on emerging visualization techniques and best practices to ensure that your visualizations remain relevant and impactful.

Engage with stakeholders throughout the process to tailor visualizations to their needs and objectives, ultimately facilitating data-driven decision-making and intelligence analysis.

Chapter 7: Cross-Platform Integration with Mitaka

Integrating Mitaka into OSINT toolchains is a strategic approach that enhances the capabilities of open-source intelligence (OSINT) practitioners by seamlessly incorporating Mitaka's versatile toolkit into their existing workflows.

OSINT toolchains are comprised of a collection of tools, techniques, and processes used to gather, process, analyze, and visualize information from various sources.

By integrating Mitaka, practitioners can leverage its specialized modules, automation features, and data analysis capabilities to streamline and enhance their OSINT operations.

To effectively integrate Mitaka into OSINT toolchains, it's essential to start with a clear understanding of your OSINT objectives and the specific tasks you wish to accomplish.

Define the scope of your OSINT operations, whether they focus on individuals, organizations, events, or trends, to guide the integration process effectively.

Mitaka offers a wide range of pre-built modules and integrations designed to interact with diverse data sources, including social media platforms, websites, and online forums.

Select the modules that align with your OSINT objectives and the sources where your target data resides.

These pre-built modules simplify the process of importing, processing, and analyzing data from various platforms.

Customization plays a pivotal role in integrating Mitaka into OSINT toolchains.

Consider developing custom modules or scripts tailored to your specific data collection and analysis requirements.

Custom modules enable you to implement specialized algorithms or techniques that may not be covered by pre-built modules, providing flexibility and depth to your toolchain.

Automation is a fundamental component of integrating Mitaka into OSINT toolchains.

Configure automated workflows that continuously monitor and collect data from your selected sources.

Automation not only saves time but also ensures that relevant data is consistently gathered, particularly in fast-paced OSINT operations.

Mitaka's real-time monitoring and alerting capabilities complement the automation process.

Set up alerts based on specific triggers, such as keywords, hashtags, or user mentions, to receive timely notifications when relevant information surfaces in your chosen data sources.

These alerts enable you to stay updated on emerging developments and respond swiftly to critical events.

Data preprocessing and cleansing are essential steps in integrating Mitaka into OSINT toolchains.

Mitaka offers tools for data cleaning, transformation, and normalization, ensuring that the data you collect is of high quality and consistency.

Clean and well-preprocessed data forms the foundation for meaningful analysis and visualization.

Advanced data analysis techniques are a valuable addition when integrating Mitaka into OSINT toolchains.

Leverage Mitaka's integration with statistical software, machine learning libraries, and data analysis tools to uncover patterns, trends, and insights within your data.

These techniques assist in identifying relationships and dependencies that may not be apparent through manual analysis.

Machine learning and artificial intelligence (AI) are powerful tools for enhancing data analysis in OSINT toolchains.

Integrate machine learning algorithms to predict outcomes, classify data, and detect anomalies within your datasets.

AI-driven techniques can uncover intricate insights that may be challenging to discover through traditional analysis methods.

Visualization is an integral part of integrating Mitaka into OSINT toolchains.

Mitaka provides visualization tools to create charts, graphs, maps, and interactive dashboards that facilitate data exploration and presentation.

Visualizations simplify complex information and communicate findings effectively to stakeholders.

Mitaka's capabilities extend to geospatial data visualization, allowing for the integration of geographic information into your toolchain.

This is particularly valuable when analyzing location-based data, such as event tracking or geospatial intelligence.

Data fusion and integration are essential when integrating Mitaka into OSINT toolchains.

Combine data from multiple sources, both within and outside Mitaka, to enrich your analysis and gain a comprehensive understanding of your subject.

Cross-referencing data enhances the reliability of your insights and reduces the risk of relying on single-source information.

Ethical considerations are paramount in OSINT, even when integrating Mitaka into toolchains.

Adhere to ethical principles, respect privacy, and handle data in compliance with data protection regulations.

Ensure that your toolchain practices align with ethical standards to maintain integrity and protect individuals' rights.

Collaboration is a valuable asset in integrating Mitaka into OSINT toolchains.

Mitaka supports multiple users working on the same OSINT project simultaneously, fostering knowledge sharing and peer review of collected data and analysis.

Collaborative efforts enhance the quality and comprehensiveness of your OSINT operations.

Regularly review and update your integration strategies to adapt to evolving data sources, analytical requirements, and stakeholder needs.

Stay informed about emerging tools, techniques, and best practices to ensure that your OSINT toolchain remains effective and relevant.

Integrating Mitaka into OSINT toolchains is an iterative process that demands continuous refinement and optimization.

In summary, integrating Mitaka into OSINT toolchains is a strategic approach that enhances the capabilities of OSINT practitioners by incorporating Mitaka's versatile toolkit into existing workflows.

Clear objectives, customization, automation, data preprocessing, advanced analysis, visualization, and ethical considerations are fundamental principles in effectively integrating Mitaka.

Collaboration and adaptability are essential elements to ensure that the integrated toolchain remains effective in dynamic OSINT operations.

By following these principles and leveraging Mitaka's capabilities, OSINT practitioners can enhance their data collection, analysis, and visualization efforts, ultimately contributing to informed decision-making and threat detection.

Leveraging Mitaka across multiple platforms is a strategic

approach that allows open-source intelligence (OSINT) practitioners to harness the full potential of Mitaka's capabilities across a variety of online sources and environments.

By doing so, practitioners can maximize their efficiency, streamline their workflows, and gain comprehensive insights from diverse data sources.

To effectively leverage Mitaka across multiple platforms, it's essential to start with a clear understanding of your OSINT objectives and the specific platforms or sources that are relevant to your investigative needs.

Identify the platforms where your target data resides, whether they are social media networks, websites, online forums, or other online communities.

Mitaka offers a range of pre-built modules and integrations designed to interact with different platforms and data sources.

Select the modules that align with your OSINT objectives and the platforms you intend to explore.

These pre-built modules simplify the process of importing, processing, and analyzing data from various online sources, reducing the complexity of data collection.

Customization is a key aspect of leveraging Mitaka across multiple platforms.

Consider developing custom modules or scripts tailored to the unique requirements of each platform or data source.

Custom modules allow you to implement specialized algorithms or techniques that cater to the specific characteristics and data structures of each platform.

Automation plays a crucial role in leveraging Mitaka across multiple platforms.

Configure automated workflows for each platform to ensure continuous data collection and monitoring.

Automation not only saves time but also enables you to stay updated on emerging information, particularly in dynamic online environments.

Mitaka's real-time monitoring and alerting capabilities complement the automation process.

Set up alerts based on specific triggers, such as keywords, hashtags, or user activities, to receive timely notifications when relevant data or events occur on the platforms you are monitoring.

These alerts enable you to respond promptly to critical developments and emerging trends.

Data preprocessing and cleansing are fundamental steps in leveraging Mitaka across multiple platforms.

Mitaka provides tools for cleaning, transforming, and normalizing data from various sources, ensuring that the data you collect is of high quality and consistency.

Well-preprocessed data enhances the accuracy and reliability of your analysis.

Advanced data analysis techniques are valuable when leveraging Mitaka across multiple platforms.

Integrate Mitaka with statistical software, machine learning libraries, and data analysis tools to uncover patterns, trends, and insights within your data.

These techniques help you extract meaningful information from the diverse data collected across different platforms.

Machine learning and artificial intelligence (AI) can further enhance your analysis when leveraging Mitaka across multiple platforms.

Integrate machine learning algorithms to automate data classification, sentiment analysis, and anomaly detection across various data sources.

AI-driven techniques can provide valuable insights and automation capabilities that streamline the analysis process.

Visualization is an essential component of leveraging Mitaka across multiple platforms.

Mitaka offers visualization tools that allow you to create charts, graphs, maps, and interactive dashboards to explore and present your findings.

Visualizations simplify complex data and enable clear communication of insights to stakeholders.

Mitaka's support for geospatial data visualization is particularly beneficial when dealing with location-based data from multiple platforms.

Geospatial visualizations help you identify geographic patterns and relationships within your data.

Data fusion and integration are essential when leveraging Mitaka across multiple platforms.

Combine data from various sources, both within and outside Mitaka, to enrich your analysis and gain a comprehensive understanding of your subject.

Cross-referencing data enhances the reliability of your insights and reduces the risk of relying on single-source information.

Ethical considerations are paramount when leveraging Mitaka across multiple platforms.

Respect privacy, adhere to data protection regulations, and handle sensitive information with care, especially when working with data from online communities and social networks.

Collaboration is a valuable asset when leveraging Mitaka across multiple platforms.

Mitaka supports collaboration among multiple users working on the same OSINT project simultaneously.

This collaboration enables knowledge sharing and peer review of collected data and analysis.

Regularly review and update your strategies for leveraging Mitaka across multiple platforms to adapt to evolving data sources, analytical requirements, and stakeholder needs.

Stay informed about emerging tools, techniques, and best practices to ensure that your OSINT efforts remain effective and relevant.

Leveraging Mitaka across multiple platforms is an iterative process that requires continuous refinement and optimization.

In summary, leveraging Mitaka across multiple platforms empowers OSINT practitioners to maximize their capabilities, streamline workflows, and gain comprehensive insights from diverse data sources.

Customization, automation, data preprocessing, advanced analysis, visualization, and ethical considerations are fundamental principles in effectively leveraging Mitaka.

Collaboration and adaptability ensure that your OSINT efforts remain effective and responsive to the evolving landscape of online platforms and data sources.

By following these principles and harnessing Mitaka's capabilities, OSINT practitioners can enhance their data collection, analysis, and visualization across a multitude of online environments, ultimately contributing to informed decision-making and threat detection.

Chapter 8: Mitaka in Red Team Operations

Mitaka plays a pivotal role in red team exercises, which are simulation-driven assessments aimed at evaluating an organization's security posture, preparedness, and vulnerabilities.

In these exercises, Mitaka serves as a versatile toolkit that enhances red team capabilities by enabling the automation, integration, and analysis of open-source intelligence (OSINT) data.

Red team exercises are essential for organizations to assess and improve their security defenses by emulating realistic threat scenarios.

Mitaka's capabilities contribute significantly to the success of red team operations by providing valuable OSINT tools and automation capabilities.

To fully understand Mitaka's role in red team exercises, it's crucial to comprehend the objectives and methodologies of such assessments.

Red team exercises involve emulating the tactics, techniques, and procedures (TTPs) of real-world adversaries to assess an organization's security posture and identify weaknesses.

These exercises are often conducted in a controlled, authorized manner to ensure that the organization's security team can evaluate and enhance their defensive capabilities.

Mitaka enhances red team exercises by automating various aspects of OSINT data collection, analysis, and reporting.

Automation is a fundamental aspect of Mitaka's role in red team exercises.

Automated workflows and modules streamline the process of gathering OSINT data, which is a critical component of red team assessments.

By automating data collection, Mitaka allows red teams to focus their efforts on analyzing and exploiting vulnerabilities, rather than spending excessive time on manual data gathering.

Furthermore, Mitaka supports real-time monitoring and alerting, allowing red teams to stay informed about emerging information that may be relevant to their objectives.

Alerts based on specific triggers, such as keywords or indicators of compromise, enable red teams to react swiftly to new developments during exercises.

Mitaka's ability to integrate with various data sources is another essential aspect of its role in red team exercises.

Red team assessments often involve collecting data from a wide range of sources, including social media, online forums, websites, and other public platforms.

Mitaka's pre-built modules and integration capabilities simplify the process of importing and processing data from diverse sources.

This integration ensures that red teams have access to a comprehensive dataset for analysis.

Mitaka's data preprocessing and cleansing tools play a crucial role in ensuring the quality and consistency of the data used in red team exercises.

Clean and well-preprocessed data is essential for accurate analysis and reliable results.

Mitaka provides tools for data cleaning, transformation, and normalization, ensuring that the data collected is reliable and suitable for analysis.

Advanced data analysis techniques are valuable when using Mitaka in red team exercises.

Red teams can leverage Mitaka's integration with statistical software, machine learning libraries, and data analysis tools to uncover patterns, trends, and insights within the OSINT data they collect.

Machine learning algorithms can help red teams identify potential vulnerabilities and prioritize their exploitation.

Visualization is another key component of Mitaka's role in red team exercises.

Mitaka offers visualization tools that allow red teams to create charts, graphs, maps, and interactive dashboards to explore and present their findings.

Visualizations simplify complex information, making it easier to communicate insights to stakeholders and decision-makers.

Geospatial data visualization, supported by Mitaka, is particularly useful for red team exercises involving location-based data, such as geospatial intelligence (GEOINT).

Data fusion and integration are essential when using Mitaka in red team exercises.

Red teams often need to combine data from multiple sources to build a comprehensive picture of the target organization's vulnerabilities and potential attack vectors.

Mitaka supports data integration, allowing red teams to combine data from various sources to create a more accurate and detailed assessment.

Ethical considerations remain crucial when Mitaka is used in red team exercises.

While the goal is to simulate real-world threats, it's essential to respect legal and ethical boundaries.

Red teams must adhere to ethical principles and legal regulations to ensure that their actions do not cause harm or violate privacy rights.

Collaboration is an essential aspect of Mitaka's role in red team exercises.

Red team assessments often involve multiple team members working together to achieve their objectives.

Mitaka supports collaboration by allowing multiple users to work on the same OSINT project simultaneously.

Collaboration enhances knowledge sharing, improves analysis, and ensures that red team efforts are coordinated effectively.

Regular review and updates of strategies for using Mitaka in red team exercises are necessary to adapt to evolving threats, data sources, and stakeholder needs.

Staying informed about emerging tools, techniques, and best practices is essential for red teams to maintain their effectiveness in conducting assessments.

Integrating Mitaka into red team exercises is an iterative process that requires ongoing refinement and optimization.

In summary, Mitaka plays a vital role in red team exercises by providing a versatile OSINT toolkit that enhances automation, integration, and analysis capabilities.

Red team exercises aim to assess and improve an organization's security posture, and Mitaka contributes significantly to their success by automating data collection, integrating diverse data sources, supporting advanced analysis, facilitating visualization, and ensuring ethical conduct.

Mitaka's role in red team exercises is crucial for identifying vulnerabilities and evaluating an organization's readiness to defend against real-world threats, ultimately contributing to enhanced security and preparedness.

Applying Mitaka in offensive open-source intelligence (OSINT) operations requires a strategic approach that leverages its capabilities for gathering, analyzing, and exploiting information from various sources.

Offensive OSINT aims to collect intelligence to gain an advantage or conduct targeted operations, making Mitaka an invaluable tool for such endeavors.

To effectively apply Mitaka in offensive OSINT, it's essential to have a clear understanding of your objectives and the targets you intend to investigate.

Define the scope of your offensive OSINT operations, whether they involve individuals, organizations, or specific events.

Mitaka offers a wide range of pre-built modules and integrations designed to interact with diverse data sources, such as social media, websites, and online forums.

Select the modules that align with your offensive OSINT objectives and the sources where your target data resides.

These pre-built modules simplify the process of importing, processing, and analyzing data from various platforms, saving you time and effort.

Customization is a crucial aspect of applying Mitaka in offensive OSINT.

Consider developing custom modules or scripts tailored to your specific data collection and analysis requirements.

Custom modules allow you to implement specialized algorithms or techniques that may not be covered by pre-built modules, giving you a competitive edge in offensive operations.

Automation plays a pivotal role in applying Mitaka in offensive OSINT.

Configure automated workflows that continuously monitor and collect data from your selected sources.

Automation not only saves time but also ensures that relevant data is consistently gathered, particularly in fast-paced offensive operations.

Mitaka's real-time monitoring and alerting capabilities complement automation by providing timely notifications based on specific triggers, such as keywords or target activities.

Set up alerts to keep you informed about emerging information relevant to your offensive objectives.

Data preprocessing and cleansing are essential when applying Mitaka in offensive OSINT.

Mitaka provides tools for data cleaning, transformation, and normalization, ensuring that the data you collect is of high quality and consistency.

Well-preprocessed data is essential for accurate analysis and decision-making in offensive operations.

Advanced data analysis techniques are invaluable when applying Mitaka in offensive OSINT.

Leverage Mitaka's integration with statistical software, machine learning libraries, and data analysis tools to uncover patterns, trends, and insights within your data.

These techniques help you identify vulnerabilities, assess risks, and prioritize targets more effectively.

Machine learning and artificial intelligence (AI) can further enhance your offensive OSINT operations.

Integrate machine learning algorithms to automate data classification, sentiment analysis, and anomaly detection, providing you with a competitive advantage in intelligence gathering.

Visualization is a critical component of applying Mitaka in offensive OSINT.

Mitaka offers visualization tools to create charts, graphs, maps, and interactive dashboards that facilitate data exploration and presentation.

Visualizations simplify complex information and enable you to communicate findings effectively to decision-makers.

Mitaka's support for geospatial data visualization is particularly valuable when conducting offensive OSINT with a geographic focus.

Data fusion and integration are crucial when applying Mitaka in offensive OSINT.

Combine data from multiple sources, both within and outside Mitaka, to enrich your analysis and gain a comprehensive understanding of your targets.

Cross-referencing data enhances the reliability of your findings and reduces the risk of relying on single-source information.

Ethical considerations remain essential in offensive OSINT operations, even when applying Mitaka.

Adhere to ethical principles, respect privacy, and handle data in compliance with legal and regulatory frameworks.

Ensure that your operations align with ethical standards to maintain integrity and protect individuals' rights.

Collaboration can be advantageous when applying Mitaka in offensive OSINT.

Mitaka supports multiple users working on the same OSINT project simultaneously, fostering knowledge sharing and peer review of collected data and analysis.

Collaborative efforts enhance the quality and comprehensiveness of your offensive operations.

Regularly review and update your strategies for applying Mitaka in offensive OSINT to adapt to evolving targets, data sources, and offensive objectives.

Stay informed about emerging tools, techniques, and best practices to maintain a competitive edge in offensive operations.

Applying Mitaka in offensive OSINT is an iterative process that demands continuous refinement and optimization.

In summary, applying Mitaka in offensive open-source intelligence (OSINT) operations requires a strategic approach that leverages its capabilities for gathering, analyzing, and exploiting information from diverse sources.

Customization, automation, data preprocessing, advanced analysis, visualization, and ethical considerations are fundamental principles when applying Mitaka in offensive OSINT.

Collaboration and adaptability are essential to ensure that offensive operations remain effective and responsive to evolving targets and threats.

By following these principles and harnessing Mitaka's capabilities, practitioners can enhance their offensive OSINT operations, ultimately contributing to informed decision-making and achieving their intelligence objectives.

Chapter 9: Mitaka for Threat Intelligence

Threat intelligence is a critical component of modern cybersecurity, and Mitaka plays a significant role in facilitating the collection, analysis, and utilization of threat intelligence data.

In the ever-evolving landscape of cyber threats, organizations need actionable information to proactively defend against potential attacks.

Mitaka's capabilities empower security professionals to gather and leverage threat intelligence effectively.

To fully grasp the importance of threat intelligence with Mitaka, it's essential to understand the concept of threat intelligence itself.

Threat intelligence encompasses the knowledge, insights, and data that help organizations identify and assess potential threats to their security.

This intelligence can come from a variety of sources, including open-source data, classified information, and proprietary databases.

Mitaka focuses primarily on open-source threat intelligence, utilizing publicly available data to provide valuable insights.

One of Mitaka's core strengths in threat intelligence is its ability to automate the collection of open-source threat data from various online sources.

This automation simplifies the process of gathering data on emerging threats, vulnerabilities, and malicious actors.

Mitaka's real-time monitoring capabilities further enhance its role in threat intelligence by providing continuous updates on relevant information.

Security professionals can configure Mitaka to monitor specific threat indicators, such as known attack patterns, malicious IP addresses, or compromised credentials, and receive immediate alerts when these indicators appear in the open-source data.

The automation of data collection and monitoring allows organizations to stay ahead of potential threats and respond more rapidly to emerging cybersecurity risks.

Mitaka's integration with various data sources is another crucial aspect of its role in threat intelligence.

Threat intelligence data can originate from a wide range of sources, including social media, forums, blogs, and government reports.

Mitaka's pre-built modules and integrations simplify the process of importing and processing data from these diverse sources.

This integration ensures that security professionals have access to a comprehensive dataset for threat analysis.

Data preprocessing is a critical step in threat intelligence, and Mitaka provides tools to clean, transform, and normalize the data collected.

Clean and well-preprocessed data is essential for accurate threat analysis, as it reduces the risk of false positives and enhances the quality of threat intelligence reports.

Advanced data analysis techniques are indispensable when dealing with threat intelligence, and Mitaka supports these capabilities.

Security professionals can leverage Mitaka's integration with statistical software, machine learning libraries, and data analysis tools to identify patterns, trends, and anomalies in threat data.

Machine learning algorithms can aid in the automatic classification of threats and the prediction of potential attack vectors.

Visualization is another essential aspect of threat intelligence with Mitaka.

Mitaka offers visualization tools that allow security professionals to create charts, graphs, and maps to represent threat data visually.

Visualizations simplify complex information and help organizations make informed decisions based on threat intelligence.

Geospatial data visualization, supported by Mitaka, is particularly valuable when assessing threats with geographic dimensions.

Threat intelligence is most effective when organizations can act on the information they receive.

Mitaka facilitates the dissemination of threat intelligence by allowing security professionals to share their findings and analysis with relevant stakeholders.

This sharing ensures that decision-makers, incident response teams, and security personnel are informed about potential threats and can take appropriate actions.

Ethical considerations remain paramount in the field of threat intelligence with Mitaka.

Security professionals must adhere to ethical principles, legal regulations, and privacy standards when collecting, analyzing, and sharing threat intelligence data.

Respecting privacy rights and protecting sensitive information are fundamental aspects of responsible threat intelligence practices.

Collaboration among security professionals is vital in the realm of threat intelligence, and Mitaka supports collaborative efforts.

Multiple team members can work together on threat intelligence projects simultaneously, sharing their expertise and insights to enhance the quality of threat analysis.

Regular reviews and updates of threat intelligence strategies are essential to adapt to evolving threats and emerging attack vectors.

Staying informed about the latest threat intelligence sources, analysis techniques, and threat actors is crucial to maintaining an effective threat intelligence program.

Mitaka's role in threat intelligence is an ongoing process that requires continuous refinement and optimization.

In summary, threat intelligence is a critical aspect of modern cybersecurity, and Mitaka serves as a powerful tool for collecting, analyzing, and utilizing open-source threat data.

Automation, integration, data preprocessing, advanced analysis, visualization, ethical considerations, collaboration, and adaptability are fundamental principles in threat intelligence with Mitaka.

By following these principles and harnessing Mitaka's capabilities, organizations can enhance their threat detection and response capabilities, ultimately bolstering their cybersecurity posture in an ever-evolving threat landscape.

Analyzing threats and vulnerabilities is a fundamental process in the realm of cybersecurity, as it helps organizations understand their risk landscape and take proactive measures to protect their assets.

In today's digital age, where cyber threats are constantly evolving, a robust analysis of threats and vulnerabilities is essential for effective cybersecurity management.

The process begins with the identification of potential threats that could harm an organization's information systems, networks, and data.

Threats can take various forms, including malware, phishing attacks, denial-of-service (DoS) attacks, insider threats, and many others.

To identify threats effectively, organizations must continually monitor their IT environments, review security incident reports, and stay informed about emerging threats in the cybersecurity landscape.

Once threats are identified, organizations need to assess their vulnerabilities - weaknesses in their systems, applications, or policies that could be exploited by threats.

Vulnerabilities can exist in software, hardware, configurations, or even human processes, making it crucial to conduct thorough vulnerability assessments.

Common vulnerability assessment techniques include penetration testing, vulnerability scanning, and code reviews.

These assessments help organizations pinpoint vulnerabilities before attackers can exploit them.

Analyzing threats and vulnerabilities involves prioritizing the identified risks based on their potential impact and likelihood of occurrence.

This process, known as risk assessment, allows organizations to focus their resources on mitigating the most critical threats and vulnerabilities first.

A risk assessment typically assigns a risk score to each identified threat and vulnerability, taking into account factors such as the potential harm it could cause and the likelihood of it being exploited.

Analyzing threats and vulnerabilities also requires organizations to consider the specific assets and data that could be targeted.

Assets may include sensitive customer information, intellectual property, financial data, and critical infrastructure.

Understanding what is at risk helps organizations tailor their security measures to protect their most valuable assets effectively.

Moreover, organizations must consider the attack vectors that could be used by threat actors to exploit vulnerabilities.

Attack vectors are pathways or methods attackers can use to gain unauthorized access to a system or network.

Understanding these vectors enables organizations to implement appropriate security controls and safeguards.

To analyze threats and vulnerabilities comprehensively, organizations can employ threat modeling techniques.

Threat modeling involves systematically evaluating an application or system's security from an attacker's perspective.

It identifies potential threats, entry points, and weak links in the security chain.

By visualizing potential attack scenarios, organizations can design more resilient security architectures and mitigation strategies.

Furthermore, organizations should continuously monitor their environments for new threats and vulnerabilities.

Cyber threats are dynamic, and new vulnerabilities can emerge with software updates, system changes, or evolving attack techniques.

Implementing an ongoing monitoring and assessment program ensures that organizations remain vigilant and can adapt their security measures accordingly.

An essential aspect of analyzing threats and vulnerabilities is the need for a collaborative approach.

Security teams, IT professionals, and business leaders must work together to identify, assess, and address risks effectively.

Cross-functional collaboration allows organizations to align their security efforts with their business objectives and prioritize resources where they are needed most.

Moreover, organizations should consider external sources of threat intelligence, such as security vendors, industry reports, and government agencies.

These sources provide valuable insights into emerging threats and vulnerabilities that may affect specific industries or technologies.

By incorporating external threat intelligence into their analysis, organizations can stay ahead of potential risks.

Analyzing threats and vulnerabilities is an ongoing process that requires continuous improvement.

Organizations should regularly update their threat and vulnerability assessments to reflect changes in their IT environments, business operations, and the threat landscape.

This iterative approach ensures that security measures remain effective and aligned with the evolving nature of cyber threats.

Once threats and vulnerabilities are identified and assessed, organizations must develop strategies to mitigate the risks effectively.

Mitigation strategies involve implementing security controls, best practices, and countermeasures to reduce the impact and likelihood of threats being realized.

Security controls can take various forms, such as firewalls, intrusion detection systems, encryption, access controls, and employee training.

The choice of security controls depends on the specific threats and vulnerabilities identified during the analysis.

It's essential to prioritize the implementation of security controls based on the risk assessment's findings.

High-risk threats and vulnerabilities should be addressed promptly with robust controls, while lower-risk items can be addressed over time.

Organizations should also establish an incident response plan to manage and respond to security incidents effectively.

Incident response plans outline the steps to take in the event of a security breach, from identifying the incident to containing it, eradicating the threat, and recovering from the incident.

By having a well-defined incident response plan in place, organizations can minimize the damage caused by security incidents and reduce downtime.

Furthermore, organizations should regularly test their security measures and incident response plans through simulated exercises and drills.

These tests help identify weaknesses in security controls and response procedures, allowing organizations to refine their strategies and better prepare for real-world threats.

Another critical aspect of mitigating threats and vulnerabilities is employee awareness and training.

Employees are often the first line of defense against threats like phishing attacks or social engineering.

Organizations should provide cybersecurity training to employees, teaching them to recognize potential threats and how to respond appropriately.

Additionally, organizations should enforce strong password policies, multi-factor authentication, and other access controls to limit the impact of insider threats.

Lastly, monitoring and continuous improvement are essential in the mitigation phase.

Organizations should regularly monitor their security controls' effectiveness and adapt them as needed to address evolving threats.

This iterative process ensures that security measures remain aligned with the current

Chapter 10: Mitaka Best Practices and Case Studies

Best practices for Mitaka users are essential to ensure efficient, secure, and productive open-source intelligence (OSINT) operations.

As Mitaka is a powerful tool with numerous capabilities, following these best practices can maximize its potential.

First and foremost, users should start by thoroughly understanding the specific needs and objectives of their OSINT operations.

A clear understanding of what information needs to be collected and analyzed is crucial to making the most of Mitaka's capabilities.

Users should also take the time to explore Mitaka's extensive documentation and resources.

This includes user manuals, tutorials, and community forums, which can provide valuable insights and tips for using the tool effectively.

Before using Mitaka for OSINT, users should ensure that they have the necessary permissions and legal rights to collect and analyze the data they require.

Compliance with data privacy laws and ethical guidelines is paramount.

Users should always respect individuals' privacy and avoid engaging in any activities that could violate legal or ethical standards.

To get started with Mitaka, users should set up their OSINT environment properly.

This includes configuring the tool, installing necessary plugins or modules, and ensuring that all dependencies are met.

A well-configured environment lays the foundation for successful OSINT operations.

It's also essential to keep Mitaka and its associated tools up to date.

Frequent updates may include bug fixes, security patches, and new features that can enhance the tool's performance and security.

Users should regularly check for updates and apply them as needed.

When using Mitaka, it's important to have a clear workflow in place.

A defined workflow helps users stay organized and ensures that all necessary steps are taken during the OSINT process.

Workflow design should consider data collection, analysis, visualization, and reporting.

Automation is one of Mitaka's strengths, and users should leverage it to streamline repetitive tasks.

Creating automated workflows for data collection, analysis, and reporting can save time and increase efficiency.

Mitaka offers a wide range of pre-built modules and integrations, but users should also consider developing custom modules when necessary.

Custom modules can be tailored to specific OSINT needs and provide more comprehensive results.

While custom modules require additional effort to develop, they can significantly enhance the depth and accuracy of OSINT operations.

Users should also be mindful of data quality.

Mitaka provides tools for data preprocessing, cleansing, and normalization.

Cleaning and preparing data before analysis ensures that the results are accurate and reliable.

In OSINT, data can come from various sources, such as websites, social media, and online forums.

Users should be proficient in data collection techniques for different sources and understand the limitations and challenges associated with each.

Mitaka's support for geospatial data is particularly valuable when conducting OSINT operations with a geographic focus.

Users should make use of geospatial data to analyze and visualize information effectively.

Throughout the OSINT process, users should maintain clear documentation of their activities.

Detailed notes and records of data sources, methodologies, and findings are essential for accountability and reporting.

Documentation also helps ensure consistency and repeatability in OSINT operations.

Mitaka users should always verify the credibility of their sources.

Cross-referencing information from multiple sources helps confirm its accuracy and reduces the risk of relying on unreliable or biased data.

Collaboration can enhance the quality and effectiveness of OSINT operations.

Users should consider working in teams or collaborating with peers to share insights, expertise, and data.

Collaborative efforts can lead to more comprehensive and accurate results.

Mitaka users should also be aware of the legal and ethical considerations surrounding OSINT.

Respecting intellectual property rights, privacy laws, and ethical guidelines is essential.

Users should avoid engaging in activities that could infringe on individuals' rights or violate legal regulations.

Incorporating ethical considerations into OSINT operations ensures that the data collected is obtained and used responsibly.

As Mitaka is a continually evolving tool, users should stay informed about updates, new features, and best practices.

Participating in Mitaka's community and engaging with other users can provide valuable insights and opportunities for learning and improvement.

Regular training and skill development are essential for Mitaka users.

Staying up-to-date with the latest OSINT techniques, tools, and methodologies is crucial for maintaining proficiency.

Users should invest time in continuous learning and skill enhancement to stay at the forefront of OSINT practices.

In summary, following best practices is essential for Mitaka users to optimize their OSINT operations effectively.

Understanding objectives, setting up a well-configured environment, automating tasks, developing custom modules, ensuring data quality, verifying sources, collaborating, and adhering to legal and ethical standards are key aspects of these best practices.

By incorporating these principles into their OSINT workflow, Mitaka users can achieve more accurate and valuable results while maintaining the highest ethical and legal standards.

Real-world case studies provide invaluable insights into the practical application of Mitaka in various OSINT scenarios, demonstrating its effectiveness and versatility.

One such case study involves a cybersecurity firm tasked with investigating a data breach at a financial institution.

The firm utilized Mitaka to gather open-source intelligence on potential threat actors, their tactics, techniques, and procedures (TTPs), and indicators of compromise (IoCs).

Mitaka's automation capabilities significantly expedited the data collection process, allowing the cybersecurity team to quickly identify the source of the breach and take immediate action to mitigate the damage.

In another case, a law enforcement agency employed Mitaka to track down a suspect involved in a series of cybercrimes.

By leveraging Mitaka's data collection and analysis tools, investigators were able to piece together a comprehensive profile of the suspect, including their online presence, communications, and digital footprint.

This information was instrumental in apprehending the individual and building a strong case for prosecution.

Mitaka's geospatial capabilities played a pivotal role in a case involving a missing person.

Search and rescue teams used Mitaka to analyze geotagged social media data and satellite imagery to pinpoint the individual's last known location.

This real-time geospatial analysis greatly expedited the search efforts, leading to the successful rescue of the missing person.

In a corporate espionage case, a multinational company employed Mitaka to investigate potential data leaks and espionage activities.

Mitaka's data collection modules combed through public forums, dark web sources, and social media platforms to identify suspicious communication patterns and leaked information.

The evidence gathered through Mitaka played a critical role in identifying the insider threat responsible for the leaks.

Mitaka also proved invaluable in a competitive analysis scenario.

A marketing agency used Mitaka to gather intelligence on rival companies' marketing strategies, technologies, and customer engagement tactics.

By analyzing data collected from competitors' websites and online advertisements, the agency gained a competitive edge and optimized its own marketing campaigns.

In a humanitarian context, Mitaka assisted an aid organization during a natural disaster response.

The organization used Mitaka to aggregate and analyze data from various sources to assess the extent of the disaster's impact, identify affected populations, and plan relief efforts.

Mitaka's real-time data analysis capabilities helped the organization allocate resources efficiently and respond effectively to the crisis.

Mitaka's cross-platform integration capabilities were put to the test in a cybersecurity incident response case.

A large enterprise with a complex IT environment faced a sophisticated cyberattack.

Mitaka seamlessly integrated with the organization's existing cybersecurity tools, allowing for rapid threat detection, containment, and remediation.

This integration helped the company mitigate the attack's impact and protect sensitive data.

In the field of financial fraud detection, Mitaka proved its worth by helping a financial institution uncover fraudulent activities.

The institution used Mitaka to analyze transaction data, cross-referencing it with open-source intelligence to identify patterns indicative of fraudulent transactions.

Mitaka's automated analysis flagged suspicious transactions, allowing the institution to halt fraudulent activities and prevent further financial losses.

Mitaka's advanced analysis and visualization capabilities aided a research institution in a study focused on tracking the spread of disinformation online.

Researchers used Mitaka to collect and analyze data from social media platforms, news websites, and blogs.

By visualizing the data, researchers gained insights into disinformation campaigns' origins, tactics, and impact, which contributed to their research findings.

In a political campaign strategy case, a political campaign team utilized Mitaka to gain a competitive edge.

Mitaka helped the team analyze public sentiment on social media, track rival candidates' messaging, and identify key influencers.

This information allowed the campaign to adjust its strategy, target specific demographics, and tailor messages for maximum impact.

In the realm of threat intelligence, Mitaka played a pivotal role in an incident involving a targeted cyberattack on a critical infrastructure organization.

Mitaka's automation capabilities continuously monitored open-source threat data, alerting the organization to emerging threats and vulnerabilities.

This real-time threat intelligence enabled the organization to proactively bolster its cybersecurity defenses and prevent potential attacks.

These real-world case studies demonstrate the diverse range of applications for Mitaka in OSINT and intelligence-related operations.

From cybersecurity and law enforcement to humanitarian aid, marketing, and research, Mitaka's capabilities have been harnessed effectively to address complex challenges and achieve successful outcomes.

BOOK 3
EXPERT OSINT STRATEGIES
HARNESSING BUILTWITH FOR PROFOUND INSIGHTS

ROB BOTWRIGHT

Chapter 1: The Power of BuiltWith in OSINT

Understanding BuiltWith's role in open-source intelligence (OSINT) is crucial for harnessing its capabilities effectively.

BuiltWith is a powerful tool that plays a pivotal role in profiling website technologies and conducting OSINT operations related to online platforms.

At its core, BuiltWith provides valuable insights into the technologies used by websites, offering a comprehensive view of their tech stacks.

These insights encompass various aspects, such as web frameworks, content management systems, server software, analytics tools, and more.

BuiltWith achieves this by scanning websites and analyzing the underlying code and server responses, providing a detailed breakdown of the technologies in use.

One of BuiltWith's primary functions in OSINT is to assist in competitive analysis.

By examining the technologies employed by competitors' websites, organizations can gain a strategic advantage.

They can identify the tools and platforms that competitors rely on for online presence, enabling them to make informed decisions about their own technology stack and digital strategy.

BuiltWith's OSINT capabilities extend to market research and trend analysis.

Organizations can use the tool to identify trends in technology adoption across industries, helping them stay ahead of the curve and align their strategies with emerging technologies.

BuiltWith also aids in lead generation, as it can uncover websites that use specific technologies or services.

This information can be valuable for sales and marketing teams seeking to target businesses that may benefit from their products or services.

Furthermore, BuiltWith contributes significantly to cybersecurity and threat intelligence efforts.

Security professionals can use the tool to identify vulnerable technologies or outdated software on websites, allowing them to proactively address security risks.

BuiltWith's data can be integrated into threat intelligence platforms to enhance the identification of potential attack vectors and vulnerabilities.

In the realm of OSINT investigations, BuiltWith can provide critical information for profiling individuals or organizations.

By analyzing the technologies associated with a target's online presence, investigators can gain insights into their digital footprint, helping to piece together a comprehensive profile.

For cybersecurity investigations, BuiltWith can reveal the technological infrastructure of malicious websites or servers.

This information is essential for understanding the threat landscape and formulating effective response strategies.

BuiltWith's role in OSINT also extends to digital marketing and e-commerce intelligence.

Marketers can use the tool to identify the marketing technologies and advertising platforms employed by competitors, allowing them to refine their marketing strategies and gain a competitive edge.

E-commerce businesses can leverage BuiltWith to analyze the technologies used by successful online retailers, helping them optimize their own e-commerce platforms.

BuiltWith's relevance in corporate investigations cannot be understated.

Investigators can use the tool to uncover hidden relationships between companies, identifying shared technologies and potential business partnerships.

This information can be crucial for due diligence and uncovering potential conflicts of interest.

BuiltWith offers a range of features that enhance its utility in OSINT.

Users can access historical data, allowing them to track technology changes on websites over time.

This feature is invaluable for trend analysis and understanding how organizations evolve their online presence.

BuiltWith also provides data exports, enabling users to save and analyze technology profiles offline.

Users can generate reports and share them with colleagues or clients, facilitating collaboration and decision-making.

Moreover, BuiltWith offers an API that allows for seamless integration with other OSINT tools and platforms.

This API empowers organizations to automate technology profiling and incorporate BuiltWith data into their existing workflows.

While BuiltWith is a powerful OSINT tool, it is essential to use it responsibly and ethically.

Users must respect website terms of service and privacy policies when collecting data with BuiltWith.

Additionally, understanding the limitations of the tool is crucial.

BuiltWith may not always accurately detect every technology used on a website, and results can vary based on factors such as website complexity and changes in technology.

To maximize BuiltWith's utility in OSINT, users should continuously update their knowledge and skills.

Staying informed about the latest features, techniques, and best practices ensures that users can harness BuiltWith's full potential effectively.

In summary, BuiltWith's role in OSINT is multifaceted and extends to various domains, including competitive analysis, market research, lead generation, cybersecurity, investigations, marketing, and e-commerce intelligence.

Its capabilities in profiling website technologies, uncovering trends, and aiding decision-making make it a valuable asset for organizations and professionals engaged in OSINT operations.

Understanding how to leverage BuiltWith's features responsibly and effectively enhances its role in open-source intelligence and contributes to more informed decision-making and strategy development.

Exploring the benefits and limitations of BuiltWith is essential for individuals and organizations looking to make informed decisions regarding its utilization in open-source intelligence (OSINT) operations.

BuiltWith's primary benefit lies in its ability to provide comprehensive insights into the technologies powering websites and online platforms.

This technology profiling feature is instrumental in competitive analysis, helping businesses gain a strategic advantage by identifying the tools and platforms employed by their competitors.

By understanding the technology stack of competitors, organizations can make informed decisions about their own digital strategies, technology adoption, and innovation.

Another significant benefit of BuiltWith is its utility in market research and trend analysis.

It enables organizations to track technology adoption trends across industries, helping them stay ahead of the curve and align their strategies with emerging technologies.

Market researchers can use BuiltWith to identify market niches with specific technology needs, allowing them to tailor their offerings accordingly.

Furthermore, BuiltWith offers a valuable advantage in lead generation.

Sales and marketing teams can utilize the tool to identify potential prospects based on their technology preferences.

This information streamlines the lead generation process, enabling teams to focus their efforts on businesses that are more likely to benefit from their products or services.

BuiltWith's role in cybersecurity is also noteworthy, as it assists in identifying vulnerabilities and security risks associated with websites and online platforms.

Security professionals can use the tool to pinpoint outdated or vulnerable technologies, helping them proactively address security threats.

BuiltWith's data can be integrated into threat intelligence platforms, enhancing the identification of potential attack vectors and vulnerabilities.

In the realm of OSINT investigations, BuiltWith serves as a valuable asset.

Investigators can leverage it to profile individuals or organizations by analyzing the technologies associated with their online presence.

This capability aids in creating comprehensive profiles and understanding the digital footprint of targets.

Moreover, BuiltWith plays a vital role in digital marketing and e-commerce intelligence.

Marketers can use the tool to gain insights into the marketing technologies, advertising platforms, and digital strategies of competitors.

This information empowers them to refine their marketing tactics and stay competitive in the online marketplace.

E-commerce businesses can benefit from BuiltWith by analyzing the technologies employed by successful online retailers.

This knowledge allows them to optimize their own e-commerce platforms and replicate the success of industry leaders.

While BuiltWith offers several advantages, it also has limitations that users should be aware of.

One limitation is its reliance on publicly available data.

BuiltWith scans websites and analyzes their publicly accessible information, which means that it may not capture proprietary or internal technologies that are not exposed to the public.

Additionally, BuiltWith may not always provide a complete and accurate picture of a website's technology stack.

The tool's accuracy can be affected by factors such as website complexity, dynamic content loading, and changes in technology.

BuiltWith's results are based on its analysis at a specific point in time and may not reflect real-time changes.

As a result, users should exercise caution and consider conducting periodic checks to ensure the accuracy of the data.

Furthermore, BuiltWith may not detect every technology used on a website, especially if technologies are obfuscated or hidden intentionally.

This limitation requires users to approach technology profiling with an understanding of potential gaps in the data.

BuiltWith's utility is also subject to the terms of service and privacy policies of websites.

Users must respect these policies and ensure that their data collection activities align with legal and ethical standards.

Building on this limitation, some websites may employ anti-scraping measures or restrictions that hinder BuiltWith's data collection capabilities.

To maximize the benefits of BuiltWith and mitigate its limitations, users should continuously update their knowledge and skills.

Staying informed about the latest features, techniques, and best practices ensures that users can make the most of BuiltWith's capabilities while adhering to ethical and legal standards.

In summary, the benefits and limitations of BuiltWith make it a valuable tool for various OSINT and intelligence-related applications.

Its strengths in technology profiling, competitive analysis, market research, lead generation, cybersecurity, investigations, digital marketing, and e-commerce intelligence offer numerous advantages.

However, users should be mindful of its limitations, including its reliance on publicly available data, potential inaccuracies, and the need to respect website policies and anti-scraping measures.

By understanding both the benefits and limitations of BuiltWith, users can make informed decisions about its integration into their OSINT workflows and intelligence operations.

Chapter 2: Advanced Techniques for BuiltWith Profiling

Delving into advanced profiling techniques is essential for those seeking to elevate their open-source intelligence (OSINT) capabilities and gain deeper insights into their targets.

While basic profiling provides valuable information, advanced profiling takes OSINT to a higher level, offering a more comprehensive understanding of individuals, organizations, or entities.

One of the fundamental aspects of advanced profiling is the exploration of interconnected relationships and associations.

Profiling individuals or organizations often involves uncovering their connections to other entities, whether through professional networks, partnerships, or affiliations.

Advanced OSINT practitioners use various techniques, such as social network analysis, to map out these relationships and identify key influencers or decision-makers within a network.

Another critical aspect of advanced profiling is the analysis of digital footprints across multiple online platforms.

Individuals and organizations leave traces of their online activities across various websites, social media platforms, forums, and online communities.

Advanced OSINT practitioners focus on aggregating and analyzing these digital footprints to gain a comprehensive view of a target's online presence.

This includes not only public profiles but also contributions, comments, and interactions within these digital spaces.

Understanding the context and sentiments associated with these interactions can provide valuable insights into a target's behavior and interests.

Advanced profiling techniques also involve deep web and dark web investigations.

While basic OSINT often focuses on publicly accessible information, advanced OSINT practitioners venture into the hidden corners of the internet to uncover concealed data.

This can include accessing password-protected forums, marketplaces, and encrypted communication channels to gather intelligence that may not be readily available on the surface web.

To navigate the deep web and dark web effectively, advanced OSINT practitioners employ anonymity and encryption tools while maintaining a thorough understanding of digital privacy and security.

Furthermore, advanced profiling extends to the analysis of sentiment and sentiment analysis tools.

Analyzing sentiments expressed in online discussions, reviews, and comments provides valuable insights into public opinion, customer satisfaction, or public perception of a target.

Advanced OSINT practitioners use sentiment analysis tools to quantify and interpret these sentiments, identifying trends, patterns, and shifts in public sentiment over time.

Additionally, advanced profiling techniques involve the utilization of advanced search operators and queries.

While basic OSINT practitioners rely on standard search queries, advanced OSINT practitioners leverage specialized search operators and techniques to narrow down results and uncover hidden information.

These operators enable users to filter and refine search queries to retrieve specific types of data or to exclude irrelevant information.

Advanced OSINT practitioners also harness the power of data enrichment and data fusion.

Data enrichment involves augmenting existing data with additional information from various sources.

Advanced OSINT practitioners seek to enhance the quality and depth of their profiles by supplementing data with details such as email addresses, phone numbers, geolocation data, and social media profiles.

Data fusion, on the other hand, involves integrating data from multiple sources to create a comprehensive picture.

By fusing data from diverse sources, advanced OSINT practitioners can connect the dots and uncover hidden insights that may not be apparent when analyzing individual data points in isolation.

Advanced profiling also requires a deep understanding of digital forensics.

Profiling often involves the examination of digital artifacts, such as metadata, file attributes, and digital signatures.

Advanced OSINT practitioners use digital forensics techniques to trace the origin and authenticity of digital content, helping to verify the credibility of information and identify potential sources.

Moreover, advanced OSINT practitioners incorporate geospatial analysis into their profiling efforts.

Geospatial analysis involves mapping and visualizing data with geographic components.

Advanced OSINT practitioners use geolocation data to track the physical movements and locations of targets, helping to paint a more accurate and detailed picture of their activities.

Additionally, advanced profiling includes linguistic analysis and natural language processing (NLP).

Language patterns, writing styles, and linguistic clues can reveal valuable information about the origin, background, or affiliations of a target.

Advanced OSINT practitioners employ NLP tools and techniques to analyze text data and extract meaningful insights from written content.

To excel in advanced profiling, practitioners must continually refine their skills in data collection, analysis, and interpretation.

They should stay updated on the latest OSINT tools and technologies, as well as the evolving landscape of digital platforms and privacy measures.

Ethical considerations remain paramount in advanced profiling, and practitioners must adhere to legal and ethical standards while conducting their investigations.

Advanced OSINT practitioners are often faced with complex challenges, but their dedication to refining their techniques and embracing advanced tools allows them to uncover valuable intelligence and provide deeper insights for decision-makers in various domains.

Fine-tuning BuiltWith is essential for OSINT practitioners seeking to harness its capabilities to conduct comprehensive technology analysis.

While BuiltWith offers powerful technology profiling features out of the box, customization and optimization are key to extracting the most valuable insights.

To fine-tune BuiltWith effectively, users should begin by understanding the specific goals of their analysis.

Each OSINT operation or investigation may have distinct objectives, and fine-tuning BuiltWith allows users to tailor their technology profiling to meet these goals.

Once the objectives are clear, users can explore BuiltWith's customization options.

One important aspect of customization is the ability to specify the depth of analysis.

Users can configure BuiltWith to conduct shallow scans for a broad overview of technologies or deep scans for a more detailed examination.

Shallow scans are useful for quickly identifying the most prevalent technologies on a website, while deep scans provide in-depth insights into each technology's configuration and usage.

Users should also consider adjusting the scanning frequency to align with their analysis needs.

Regular scans can track changes in a website's technology stack over time, making them ideal for monitoring competitors or tracking technology trends.

On the other hand, one-time scans may suffice for static analysis in certain investigations.

Another key customization option is the ability to filter and focus on specific types of technologies.

BuiltWith allows users to select technology categories or even individual technologies for analysis.

For example, users can narrow their focus to content management systems, e-commerce platforms, or advertising networks, depending on their investigative objectives.

Furthermore, BuiltWith provides the flexibility to choose the scope of analysis.

Users can target specific website sections or directories, which is particularly valuable for analyzing complex websites with diverse technology usage.

Customizing the scope ensures that the analysis is relevant to the specific area of interest.

Additionally, BuiltWith allows users to configure alerts and notifications.

By setting up alerts for changes in a website's technology stack, users can receive timely updates when new technologies are detected or existing ones are modified.

This feature is valuable for competitive analysis and tracking the adoption of emerging technologies.

Fine-tuning BuiltWith also involves optimizing data export and integration options.

Users can export technology profiles and data in various formats, including CSV and JSON, enabling seamless integration with other OSINT tools or platforms.

Integration with data visualization tools and dashboards can enhance the presentation and interpretation of technology profiling results.

Advanced users may even consider scripting or automating BuiltWith scans using the BuiltWith API, allowing for greater customization and integration into existing workflows.

Furthermore, users should pay attention to BuiltWith's data sources and coverage.

BuiltWith relies on a vast database of websites and technologies, but the comprehensiveness of its data can vary. Users should be aware of potential gaps in coverage, especially for less common or niche technologies.

Cross-referencing BuiltWith's findings with other OSINT tools or manual research can help fill any data gaps. To fine-tune BuiltWith effectively, users should also consider the privacy and ethical implications of their analysis.

Respecting website terms of service and privacy policies is paramount when conducting scans with BuiltWith.

Users should ensure that their scanning activities align with legal and ethical standards, avoiding any activities that may infringe on privacy or violate terms of use.

Moreover, it is essential to keep BuiltWith and its associated tools up to date.

Regularly checking for updates and improvements ensures that users have access to the latest features and technology profiling capabilities.

Fine-tuning BuiltWith is an ongoing process that requires a deep understanding of technology profiling, data analysis, and customization.

To master this tool, users should continually refine their skills and explore its advanced features.

Moreover, collaboration and knowledge sharing within the OSINT community can provide valuable insights and best practices for optimizing BuiltWith for comprehensive analysis.

In summary, fine-tuning BuiltWith for comprehensive technology analysis is a crucial step for OSINT practitioners looking to extract valuable insights from websites and online platforms.

Customization options, such as specifying the depth of analysis, filtering technologies, configuring alerts, and optimizing data export, allow users to tailor their analysis to specific investigative objectives.

Respecting privacy and ethical considerations is essential, and staying up to date with BuiltWith's features and updates ensures that users can leverage its full potential effectively.

By continually refining their skills and collaborating with peers, OSINT practitioners can fine-tune BuiltWith to enhance their technology profiling capabilities and provide deeper insights for their intelligence operations.

Chapter 3: Extracting Hidden Gems with BuiltWith

Uncovering valuable insights is the ultimate goal of open-source intelligence (OSINT) practitioners, and it requires a combination of skills, techniques, and tools.

While the world of OSINT is vast and multifaceted, the journey to uncovering valuable insights often starts with a clear understanding of the objectives.

Whether it's gathering intelligence on a target individual, organization, or online community, having well-defined goals is essential.

These objectives serve as a guiding light, directing the practitioner's efforts and informing the selection of the most appropriate OSINT methods.

In the quest for insights, OSINT practitioners frequently turn to the internet as a treasure trove of information.

The web is an expansive landscape, teeming with data in various forms, from text and images to audio and video.

To navigate this terrain effectively, practitioners employ advanced search operators and queries to sift through the digital haystack and locate the proverbial needles of information.

Search engines like Google and specialized OSINT tools play a pivotal role in this process, enabling users to refine their searches and retrieve targeted results.

Moreover, social media platforms are a rich source of insights, offering a window into the thoughts, behaviors, and interactions of individuals and groups.

By monitoring social media profiles and conversations, OSINT practitioners can gain valuable context and discern patterns of behavior.

This knowledge can be instrumental in understanding the motives, affiliations, and sentiments of their subjects.

In addition to traditional web searches and social media monitoring, OSINT practitioners often delve into the deep web and dark web.

These hidden corners of the internet house a myriad of unindexed or encrypted content that may hold critical clues.

However, venturing into these realms requires a deep understanding of digital anonymity and privacy, as well as the ability to navigate securely.

OSINT tools designed for deep web investigations can aid in this pursuit.

Beyond the digital realm, the physical world also offers opportunities for uncovering insights.

Geospatial analysis, for instance, involves examining geographic data to map out locations, movements, and connections.

By analyzing geolocation data from photos, social media posts, or online mentions, OSINT practitioners can paint a vivid picture of a subject's movements and associations.

Digital forensics techniques come into play when examining digital artifacts for hidden information.

Metadata, timestamps, and file attributes can offer critical details about the origin, manipulation, or authenticity of digital content.

These insights can be pivotal in verifying the credibility of data and tracing its source.

Language analysis and sentiment analysis provide additional layers of understanding.

By dissecting the language patterns, writing styles, and sentiments expressed in texts or communications, OSINT practitioners can uncover insights into an individual's background, motivations, or affiliations.

Natural language processing (NLP) tools aid in automating this analysis and extracting meaningful information from vast amounts of text.

As OSINT practitioners gather information from various sources, the process of data fusion becomes essential.

Data fusion involves integrating data from multiple sources to create a holistic view of the subject.

This holistic perspective allows practitioners to connect the dots and identify relationships, patterns, and anomalies that may not be evident when examining individual data points in isolation.

Moreover, OSINT practitioners utilize data enrichment techniques to augment existing data with additional details.

This might include enriching a target's profile with email addresses, phone numbers, or social media profiles to create a more comprehensive picture.

The power of OSINT lies not only in data collection but also in data analysis.

Analytical tools and methodologies aid practitioners in making sense of the collected data, distilling it into actionable insights.

These insights may pertain to a target's intentions, affiliations, vulnerabilities, or potential risks.

Ultimately, the art of uncovering valuable insights in OSINT requires a combination of technical expertise, critical thinking, and creativity.

It involves not only the adept use of tools and techniques but also a deep understanding of the subject matter and the ability to think outside the box.

Moreover, ethical considerations play a vital role in the OSINT journey.

Practitioners must adhere to legal and ethical standards, respecting privacy, consent, and the terms of service of the platforms they explore.

While the pursuit of insights can be exhilarating, it should always be conducted responsibly and with integrity.

As OSINT continues to evolve, practitioners must remain adaptable and open to new methods and technologies.

The field of OSINT is dynamic, and staying current with emerging tools and trends is essential for maintaining effectiveness.

Furthermore, collaboration within the OSINT community fosters knowledge sharing and enhances the collective ability to uncover valuable insights.

Through the exchange of experiences, best practices, and lessons learned, practitioners can continuously refine their skills and contribute to the advancement of the field.

In summary, uncovering valuable insights in the realm of OSINT is both an art and a science.

It requires a multifaceted approach that encompasses data collection, analysis, and interpretation.

The journey begins with well-defined objectives and the selection of appropriate tools and techniques.

As practitioners navigate the digital and physical landscapes, they must exercise ethical diligence and stay adaptable in an ever-evolving field.

Ultimately, the pursuit of insights in OSINT is a rewarding endeavor that contributes to informed decision-making and understanding in various domains, from cybersecurity and law enforcement to competitive intelligence and research.

Finding the unseen is the essence of open-source intelligence (OSINT), and BuiltWith is a potent tool in this endeavor.

While the internet is replete with visible information, much of what is valuable remains hidden beneath the surface.

BuiltWith serves as a key that unlocks the door to this hidden realm.

At its core, BuiltWith is a technology profiling tool that enables OSINT practitioners to uncover the technological infrastructure behind websites and online platforms.

However, its capabilities extend far beyond a simple enumeration of technologies.

BuiltWith excels in revealing the unseen by providing insights into a website's ecosystem, technology stack, and digital fingerprint.

To harness BuiltWith effectively, practitioners must first understand its fundamental components.

The heart of BuiltWith's functionality lies in its ability to detect and analyze technologies employed by websites.

These technologies encompass a wide spectrum, including content management systems, web frameworks, analytics tools, advertising networks, and more.

BuiltWith scans websites and identifies the technologies in use, compiling a comprehensive report that outlines each technology's presence, usage, and configurations.

The tool excels in categorizing and categorizing these technologies, making it easy to discern the building blocks of a website.

Furthermore, BuiltWith offers a historical perspective by tracking technology changes over time.

Practitioners can observe when technologies were first detected, when they were last seen, and how they have evolved.

This historical data is invaluable for tracking a website's technological journey and understanding the dynamics of its digital transformation.

BuiltWith's capabilities extend to competitive analysis, allowing practitioners to compare the technological profiles of multiple websites.

By benchmarking a target website against competitors or peers, practitioners gain insights into industry trends, best practices, and areas of differentiation.

This competitive intelligence aids in strategic decision-making and identifying opportunities for improvement.

Moreover, BuiltWith excels in uncovering hidden technologies and services that may not be immediately visible.

Many websites employ third-party scripts, widgets, or services that are loaded dynamically, making them challenging to detect through manual inspection.

BuiltWith's deep scanning capabilities reveal these hidden technologies, shedding light on the full scope of a website's digital infrastructure.

BuiltWith's prowess extends to tracking the usage of e-commerce and marketing technologies.

Practitioners can delve into a website's e-commerce stack, identifying the platforms, payment gateways, and shopping cart solutions in use.

This information is valuable for competitive analysis, market research, and understanding an organization's online sales strategy.

Marketing technologies, such as email marketing services, advertising pixels, and tracking tools, are also unveiled by BuiltWith.

Uncovering the unseen marketing stack of a website provides insights into its digital marketing strategies and customer engagement tactics.

BuiltWith's capabilities are not limited to the surface web.

It extends its reach into the deep web, where many websites host sensitive information or databases.

By scanning and profiling deep web pages and directories, BuiltWith helps practitioners uncover hidden data and assets that may not be indexed by search engines.

This capability is particularly relevant for cybersecurity investigations, as it aids in identifying potential vulnerabilities or data leaks.

Beyond technology profiling, BuiltWith provides geolocation data that can be pivotal in OSINT operations.

The tool reveals the physical locations of servers hosting a website, allowing practitioners to map out the geographical footprint of an organization.

This information is valuable for geospatial analysis, tracking the movements of online entities, and understanding the global distribution of digital assets.

Furthermore, BuiltWith excels in enriching data through integration with other OSINT tools and services.

Practitioners can enhance the depth and quality of their investigations by combining BuiltWith's insights with data from sources like WHOIS records, domain intelligence platforms, and social media profiles.

This data fusion enables practitioners to connect the dots and build a more comprehensive picture of a target's digital presence.

To utilize BuiltWith effectively, practitioners should adopt a systematic approach.

They must begin with clear objectives, defining the specific insights they seek to uncover.

Whether it's profiling a competitor, analyzing a potential partner, or assessing a cybersecurity risk, having a well-defined goal is essential.

Once the objectives are established, practitioners can configure BuiltWith to conduct scans tailored to their needs.

This includes specifying the depth of analysis, selecting the technology categories of interest, and defining the scope of the scan.

The tool offers flexibility in customization, allowing practitioners to focus on specific aspects of a website's technological landscape.

Practitioners can also leverage BuiltWith's alerts and notification features to monitor changes in a website's technology stack over time.

This real-time tracking is valuable for staying updated on a target's technological shifts and adaptations.

Moreover, BuiltWith provides data export options, enabling practitioners to export technology profiles and insights in various formats.

This data can be integrated into analytical workflows, reports, or dashboards, enhancing the presentation and interpretation of findings.

Additionally, BuiltWith offers an API that allows for seamless integration into existing OSINT toolchains and automation workflows.

Practitioners with advanced technical skills can script or automate scans, ensuring a continuous flow of technology profiling data.

While BuiltWith is a powerful tool, ethical considerations are paramount in its usage.

Practitioners must respect the terms of service and privacy policies of websites they scan.

Unauthorized or excessive scanning can potentially disrupt a website's operations or violate legal and ethical standards.

Moreover, practitioners should exercise discretion in handling sensitive information and data uncovered by BuiltWith.

Ensuring data security and privacy is essential, especially when dealing with personally identifiable information or confidential data.

In summary, BuiltWith's capabilities for uncovering the unseen make it a valuable asset in the OSINT toolkit.

By profiling technologies, tracking changes over time, exploring the deep web, and enriching data, BuiltWith aids practitioners in revealing hidden insights that are crucial for informed decision-making.

When used responsibly and ethically, BuiltWith empowers OSINT practitioners to uncover the technological landscapes of websites and online platforms, offering a wealth of valuable information that might otherwise remain unseen.

Chapter 4: BuiltWith and E-commerce Intelligence

E-commerce profiling with BuiltWith is a powerful application of this technology profiling tool that offers deep insights into the digital storefronts of online businesses.

Understanding the e-commerce technology stack of a website is essential for competitive analysis, market research, and strategic decision-making.

BuiltWith excels in unraveling the intricacies of e-commerce platforms, payment gateways, shopping cart solutions, and other related technologies.

To embark on e-commerce profiling, practitioners must begin by defining their objectives and the specific insights they seek to uncover.

Whether it's assessing a competitor's online sales strategy, identifying market trends, or evaluating the security posture of an e-commerce site, having clear goals is crucial.

BuiltWith provides the means to dissect the e-commerce stack of a website comprehensively.

The tool scans and identifies the e-commerce technologies in use, generating a detailed report that outlines each component's presence, configuration, and usage.

This report serves as a valuable resource for practitioners seeking to gain a deeper understanding of a target e-commerce website.

One of the primary components of e-commerce profiling is the examination of the content management system (CMS) employed by the website.

BuiltWith detects the CMS in use, whether it's a popular platform like WooCommerce, Shopify, Magento, or a custom-built solution.

Knowing the CMS is foundational, as it provides insights into the website's capabilities, flexibility, and scalability.

It also helps practitioners assess the level of customization and control that the website owner has over their online store.

Beyond the CMS, practitioners delve into the specifics of the e-commerce platform, such as the shopping cart solution.

BuiltWith identifies whether the website uses standard shopping carts or if it has implemented custom solutions tailored to its unique requirements.

Understanding the shopping cart technology is essential for evaluating the website's user experience, checkout process, and payment handling.

Moreover, payment gateways play a critical role in e-commerce operations, and BuiltWith reveals the payment solutions in use.

This information is valuable for assessing the payment options available to customers, as well as the security measures implemented for financial transactions.

Practitioners also examine the presence of security certificates and protocols, such as SSL/TLS encryption.

BuiltWith uncovers whether a website has implemented secure connections, which is essential for safeguarding sensitive customer data during online transactions.

Additionally, e-commerce profiling extends to the identification of analytics and tracking tools used by the website.

BuiltWith detects the presence of tools like Google Analytics, Facebook Pixel, and others that enable businesses to monitor user behavior, track conversions, and optimize marketing efforts.

This insight into analytics and tracking tools allows practitioners to understand the website's data-driven decision-making and marketing strategies.

Marketing technologies are a significant aspect of e-commerce profiling, as they shed light on a website's customer engagement tactics.

BuiltWith identifies email marketing services, advertising pixels, and retargeting solutions employed by the website.

This information is pivotal for assessing the effectiveness of the website's marketing campaigns and understanding its customer engagement and retention strategies.

E-commerce profiling also involves uncovering third-party integrations and services that enhance the functionality of the online store.

Many e-commerce websites integrate with third-party services for functions like shipping, inventory management, or customer support.

BuiltWith's deep scanning capabilities reveal these integrations, allowing practitioners to understand the website's ecosystem of services and partners.

Practitioners should not overlook the examination of customer reviews and ratings on e-commerce websites.

These reviews provide insights into customer satisfaction, product quality, and the overall shopping experience.

BuiltWith can aid in identifying and monitoring the presence of review management and feedback collection tools.

Moreover, e-commerce profiling encompasses geolocation data, which is valuable for understanding the global reach of an online business.

BuiltWith reveals the physical locations of servers hosting the website, providing insights into its server infrastructure and distribution.

This information is pivotal for geospatial analysis, tracking the movements of online entities, and understanding the website's geographical footprint.

To utilize BuiltWith effectively for e-commerce profiling, practitioners should adopt a structured approach.

They must define their objectives clearly, outlining the specific insights they aim to extract from the target e-commerce website.

Whether it's benchmarking a competitor's e-commerce stack, evaluating the security posture, or assessing market trends, having well-defined goals is paramount.

Once the objectives are established, practitioners can configure BuiltWith to conduct scans tailored to their needs.

This includes specifying the depth of analysis, focusing on e-commerce technology categories, and defining the scope of the scan.

BuiltWith offers customization options that allow practitioners to extract the most relevant information for their e-commerce profiling efforts.

Furthermore, practitioners can leverage BuiltWith's data export capabilities to export e-commerce technology profiles and insights in various formats.

This data can be integrated into reports, presentations, or analytical dashboards, enhancing the depth and clarity of findings.

For advanced users, BuiltWith offers an API that facilitates seamless integration into existing toolchains and workflows.

This enables practitioners to automate e-commerce profiling processes and ensure a continuous flow of data.

While e-commerce profiling with BuiltWith is a powerful tool, ethical considerations are of utmost importance.

Practitioners must respect the terms of service and privacy policies of websites they scan.

Unauthorized or excessive scanning can potentially disrupt a website's operations or violate legal and ethical standards.

Moreover, practitioners should handle any sensitive information or data uncovered by BuiltWith with care, ensuring data security and privacy.

In summary, e-commerce profiling with BuiltWith is a valuable application of technology profiling in the field of open-source intelligence (OSINT).

By dissecting the e-commerce technology stack, payment gateways, marketing technologies, and security measures, practitioners gain critical insights into online businesses.

These insights inform competitive analysis, market research, and strategic decision-making, empowering practitioners to make informed choices in the dynamic world of e-commerce.

When conducted responsibly and ethically, e-commerce profiling with BuiltWith aids OSINT practitioners in uncovering the unseen aspects of online businesses' digital storefronts, offering a wealth of valuable information that enhances their understanding and decision-making capabilities.

Leveraging BuiltWith for market research is an indispensable strategy for staying competitive and informed in today's digital landscape.

Market research is a vital component of business strategy, enabling organizations to make informed decisions, identify opportunities, and understand their competitive position.

BuiltWith provides a unique and comprehensive approach to market research by uncovering the technological landscapes of competitors and industry players.

To harness the full potential of BuiltWith for market research, practitioners must begin with a clear understanding of their objectives.

Whether it's benchmarking against competitors, identifying emerging technologies, or gauging market trends, having well-defined goals is essential.

BuiltWith's capabilities for technology profiling extend to market research, enabling practitioners to dissect the technological infrastructure of industry leaders and rivals.

One of the fundamental aspects of market research with BuiltWith is the identification of the content management systems (CMS) in use.

BuiltWith detects the CMS employed by websites, whether it's a widely-used platform like WordPress, Joomla, or a custom-built solution.

Understanding the CMS landscape of competitors and industry leaders provides insights into their web development strategies, content management capabilities, and scalability.

Moreover, practitioners delve into the specifics of e-commerce platforms to assess online businesses' market presence.

BuiltWith reveals the presence of e-commerce solutions, payment gateways, and shopping cart technologies, which are pivotal for evaluating an organization's online sales strategy and competitive position.

This information aids in understanding market trends, customer preferences, and the level of investment that competitors are making in their e-commerce infrastructure.

In addition to e-commerce technologies, BuiltWith uncovers marketing tools and analytics platforms employed by organizations.

Identifying the marketing technologies in use sheds light on their digital marketing strategies, customer engagement tactics, and data-driven decision-making.

Practitioners gain insights into the tools organizations leverage to analyze user behavior, track conversions, and optimize marketing efforts.

BuiltWith also excels in revealing the integration of third-party services and partners in an organization's technology stack.

Many companies collaborate with external providers for functions like customer support, analytics, and content delivery.

BuiltWith's deep scanning capabilities unveil these integrations, allowing practitioners to understand an organization's ecosystem of services and partners.

Market research extends to the examination of cybersecurity measures and security certificates employed by industry players.

BuiltWith identifies whether websites implement secure connections using SSL/TLS encryption, providing insights into their commitment to data security and privacy.

This information is valuable for assessing the level of trustworthiness that organizations convey to their customers and partners.

Furthermore, practitioners can examine the geolocation data provided by BuiltWith to gain insights into the geographical reach of organizations.

Understanding the physical locations of servers and data centers offers valuable information for market research, especially for businesses with global operations.

This data aids in geospatial analysis, tracking the movements of organizations, and assessing their global footprint.

To conduct effective market research with BuiltWith, practitioners must adopt a structured approach.

They should begin by clearly defining their objectives and the specific insights they aim to extract from competitors and industry leaders.

Whether it's assessing market share, understanding technological trends, or evaluating security postures, having well-defined goals guides the research process.

Once the objectives are established, practitioners can configure BuiltWith to conduct scans tailored to their market research needs.

This includes specifying the depth of analysis, focusing on technology categories of interest, and defining the scope of the scan.

BuiltWith offers customization options that enable practitioners to extract the most relevant information for their market research efforts.

Moreover, practitioners can take advantage of BuiltWith's data export capabilities to export technology profiles and insights in various formats.

This data can be integrated into market research reports, presentations, or dashboards, enhancing the quality and depth of findings.

For advanced users, BuiltWith offers an API that facilitates seamless integration into existing market research workflows and toolchains.

This allows practitioners to automate the collection of technology profiling data, ensuring that their market research is up-to-date and continuously monitored.

While BuiltWith is a powerful tool for market research, ethical considerations are paramount.

Practitioners must respect the terms of service and privacy policies of websites they scan, ensuring that their research activities comply with legal and ethical standards.

Unauthorized or excessive scanning can disrupt a website's operations and potentially lead to legal consequences.

Furthermore, practitioners should handle any sensitive information or data uncovered by BuiltWith with care, safeguarding data security and privacy.

In summary, leveraging BuiltWith for market research offers a strategic advantage in today's digital business landscape.

By profiling technologies, e-commerce solutions, marketing tools, and security measures employed by competitors and industry leaders, practitioners gain a deeper understanding of the market dynamics and trends.

These insights empower organizations to make informed decisions, identify growth opportunities, and maintain a competitive edge.

When conducted responsibly and ethically, market research with BuiltWith provides valuable intelligence that guides business strategies and ensures relevance in a rapidly evolving market.

Chapter 5: BuiltWith for Competitive Analysis

Gaining the competitive edge in today's fast-paced and ever-evolving business landscape requires a strategic and informed approach. Businesses must continually strive to stay ahead of the competition, innovate, and adapt to changing market dynamics.

To gain a competitive edge, organizations must first recognize the importance of in-depth market research.

Understanding the market, customer preferences, and emerging trends is the foundation of informed decision-making. Market research allows businesses to identify gaps in the market, assess customer needs, and uncover opportunities for growth.

A comprehensive market research strategy involves analyzing industry trends, competitor behavior, and consumer feedback. By studying market trends, organizations can anticipate shifts in demand, identify emerging technologies, and position themselves to capitalize on these changes. Competitor analysis is equally crucial in gaining a competitive edge.

Studying competitors' strategies, strengths, and weaknesses provides valuable insights into the market landscape.

Organizations can learn from competitors' successes and failures, helping them refine their own strategies.

Identifying gaps or areas where competitors may be lacking allows businesses to offer unique solutions and stand out in the market. Customer feedback is a goldmine of information for gaining a competitive edge.

Listening to customer complaints, suggestions, and preferences can guide product development and service improvements.

Implementing customer feedback can enhance product quality, customer satisfaction, and loyalty.

In addition to market research, innovation is a key driver of competitiveness. Businesses must continually innovate to create products or services that meet evolving customer needs and expectations.

Innovation can take various forms, from product enhancements to process improvements and even disruptive technologies. Organizations that foster a culture of innovation are more likely to stay ahead of the competition.

Furthermore, embracing technology is essential for gaining a competitive edge.

Technology has become a cornerstone of modern business operations. Adopting the latest technology tools and solutions can streamline processes, reduce costs, and improve efficiency. Whether it's implementing cloud computing, artificial intelligence, or data analytics, technology can provide a competitive advantage.

Effective marketing and branding are also crucial components of gaining a competitive edge.

A strong brand identity, coupled with targeted marketing strategies, can help organizations connect with their target audience. Effective marketing campaigns can create brand awareness, drive customer engagement, and boost sales.

Customer service excellence is another avenue for gaining a competitive edge. Providing exceptional customer service can set a business apart from its competitors.

A satisfied and loyal customer base can be a valuable asset, leading to repeat business and positive word-of-mouth referrals. Moreover, businesses should explore strategic partnerships and collaborations to enhance their competitive position.

Partnering with complementary businesses can extend a company's reach, access new markets, and leverage shared resources.

Collaborations can lead to innovative product offerings and mutually beneficial relationships.

Gaining a competitive edge also involves an understanding of financial management.

Effective financial planning, budgeting, and resource allocation are essential for sustaining competitiveness.

Monitoring financial performance and making data-driven decisions are critical components of financial management.

Employee development and talent acquisition are key factors in gaining a competitive edge.

A skilled and motivated workforce can drive innovation, productivity, and customer satisfaction.

Investing in employee training and development can lead to a more capable and adaptable team.

Additionally, organizations should focus on sustainability and corporate social responsibility.

Consumers increasingly value businesses that demonstrate a commitment to environmental and social causes.

Incorporating sustainable practices and ethical principles into business operations can enhance reputation and customer loyalty.

Continuous monitoring of the competitive landscape is essential for maintaining a competitive edge.

Markets are dynamic, and competitors can quickly change strategies or introduce new offerings.

Organizations must stay vigilant, adapt to market shifts, and be prepared to adjust their own strategies accordingly.

Benchmarking against industry leaders and best practices can provide insights into areas for improvement.

Finally, gaining a competitive edge requires a customer-centric approach.

Understanding customer needs, preferences, and pain points is paramount.

Organizations should regularly solicit feedback, conduct surveys, and use data analytics to gain deeper customer insights.

By aligning strategies and innovations with customer expectations, businesses can create unique value propositions and solidify their competitive position.

In summary, gaining a competitive edge is an ongoing process that involves a multifaceted approach.

It requires a commitment to market research, innovation, technology adoption, effective marketing, exceptional customer service, strategic partnerships, financial management, employee development, sustainability, and a customer-centric mindset.

By embracing these principles and continually adapting to the changing business landscape, organizations can position themselves for long-term success and competitiveness. Analyzing a competitor's tech stack with BuiltWith can provide valuable insights into their digital infrastructure and technological choices. Understanding the technologies your competitors employ is crucial for staying competitive in today's digital landscape.

BuiltWith is a powerful tool that enables you to gain a comprehensive view of the tools and technologies your competitors use on their websites.

By dissecting their tech stack, you can identify their strengths, weaknesses, and potential areas for improvement.

The first step in analyzing a competitor's tech stack is to select your target competitor.

Choose a competitor whose digital presence and online strategies closely align with your own business goals and objectives.

Once you've identified your target, use BuiltWith to perform a comprehensive scan of their website.

BuiltWith will reveal a detailed breakdown of the technologies in use, including content management systems, e-commerce platforms, web frameworks, and more.

This information can be invaluable for benchmarking your own digital strategy against theirs.

Start by examining the content management system (CMS) your competitor is using.

BuiltWith will provide insights into whether they are using popular CMS platforms like WordPress, Drupal, or Joomla, or if they have a custom-built solution.

Understanding their CMS choice can offer insights into the level of flexibility and scalability they have in managing their online content.

Next, delve into their e-commerce technology stack.

BuiltWith can identify the e-commerce platform, payment gateways, and shopping cart solutions they employ.

This information is crucial for evaluating their online sales strategy, user experience, and payment processing capabilities.

Comparing their e-commerce stack to your own can help you identify gaps or areas where you can improve.

Take note of any marketing technologies and analytics tools your competitor uses.

BuiltWith can reveal the presence of tools like Google Analytics, Facebook Pixel, and marketing automation platforms.

This information can provide insights into their data-driven decision-making and customer engagement strategies.

Understanding the tools they use for analytics and tracking can help you fine-tune your own marketing efforts.

BuiltWith also detects third-party integrations and services that your competitor may have implemented.

These integrations can range from customer support chatbots to email marketing platforms and CRM systems.

Identifying these integrations can give you a better understanding of how they manage customer interactions and data.

Assess the security measures employed by your competitor's website.

BuiltWith can reveal whether they have implemented SSL/TLS encryption, security certificates, and other security protocols.

Understanding their commitment to data security can help you evaluate their trustworthiness in the eyes of customers.

BuiltWith also provides geolocation data, which can help you assess the global reach of your competitor.

By knowing the physical locations of their servers, you can gain insights into their server infrastructure and distribution.

This information can be valuable for understanding their geographical footprint and target markets.

To effectively analyze your competitor's tech stack with BuiltWith, you must take a structured approach.

Start by defining your objectives for the analysis.

What specific insights are you seeking to gain from your competitor's tech stack?

Whether it's benchmarking against them, identifying technological trends, or evaluating their security posture, having clear goals is essential.

Configure BuiltWith to perform scans tailored to your objectives.

Specify the depth of analysis, focus on technology categories of interest, and define the scope of the scan.

BuiltWith offers customization options that allow you to extract the most relevant information for your analysis.

Leverage BuiltWith's data export capabilities to export the technology profiles and insights in various formats.

This data can be integrated into reports, presentations, or analytical dashboards to enhance the depth and clarity of your findings.

For advanced users, consider utilizing BuiltWith's API for seamless integration into your existing toolchains and workflows.

This can enable you to automate the analysis process and ensure that your competitor's tech stack is continuously monitored.

While analyzing a competitor's tech stack with BuiltWith is a powerful strategy, it's essential to approach it with ethical considerations in mind.

Respect the terms of service and privacy policies of the websites you scan.

Unauthorized or excessive scanning can potentially disrupt a website's operations or violate legal and ethical standards.

Handle any sensitive information or data uncovered by BuiltWith with care, ensuring data security and privacy.

In summary, analyzing a competitor's tech stack with BuiltWith is a strategic approach to gaining insights into their digital infrastructure and technological choices.

By understanding their CMS, e-commerce stack, marketing tools, security measures, and global reach, you can benchmark your own digital strategy and identify areas for improvement.

When conducted responsibly and ethically, this analysis can help you stay competitive in the ever-evolving digital landscape and make informed decisions to advance your business objectives.

Chapter 6: BuiltWith and Cybersecurity Investigations

Building cybersecurity profiles is an essential aspect of modern digital strategy and risk management.

In today's interconnected world, where data breaches and cyberattacks are prevalent, understanding and managing cybersecurity risks are paramount.

A cybersecurity profile is a comprehensive overview of an organization's cybersecurity measures, practices, and protocols.

It provides insights into the organization's commitment to safeguarding data, protecting sensitive information, and mitigating cybersecurity threats.

Building a cybersecurity profile begins with a thorough assessment of an organization's digital assets, including hardware, software, networks, and data repositories.

This assessment involves identifying all critical assets and classifying them based on their importance and sensitivity.

Critical assets can include customer data, financial records, intellectual property, and proprietary software.

Once assets are identified and classified, the next step is to assess potential vulnerabilities and threats.

This involves conducting vulnerability assessments, penetration testing, and risk assessments to identify weaknesses in the organization's cybersecurity posture.

Identifying vulnerabilities is crucial as it allows organizations to prioritize and address the most critical security risks.

Cyber threats are continually evolving, and organizations must stay informed about emerging threats and attack vectors.

The cybersecurity profile should include information about the organization's threat intelligence capabilities and its ability to monitor and respond to cyber threats.

This includes the use of security information and event management (SIEM) systems, intrusion detection systems (IDS), and threat intelligence feeds.

In addition to vulnerabilities and threats, the cybersecurity profile should also cover the organization's security policies and procedures.

These policies outline the rules and guidelines that employees and stakeholders must follow to maintain a secure digital environment.

Security policies should address areas such as access control, data encryption, incident response, and employee training.

To build an effective cybersecurity profile, organizations must also consider compliance with industry regulations and data protection laws.

Compliance is a critical aspect of cybersecurity, and organizations must demonstrate adherence to relevant regulations, such as GDPR, HIPAA, or PCI DSS.

The cybersecurity profile should include details about the organization's compliance efforts, including regular audits, assessments, and certifications.

Another essential component of the cybersecurity profile is the incident response plan.

This plan outlines the procedures and protocols that the organization will follow in the event of a cybersecurity incident or data breach.

It includes steps for containing the incident, notifying affected parties, and restoring normal operations.

The incident response plan should be regularly tested and updated to ensure its effectiveness.

The cybersecurity profile should also provide insights into the organization's security awareness and training programs.

Employee education and training are vital for preventing cyber threats such as phishing attacks and social engineering.

The profile should include details about the frequency of training, the topics covered, and the methods used for training employees.

Security awareness programs can significantly enhance an organization's cybersecurity posture.

The cybersecurity profile should also cover the organization's access control measures.

Access control ensures that only authorized individuals can access sensitive data and systems.

This includes the use of strong authentication methods, password policies, and role-based access controls.

Organizations should also have a strategy for monitoring and auditing user access to detect unauthorized or suspicious activities.

In addition to access control, the cybersecurity profile should provide information about the organization's data encryption practices.

Data encryption is essential for protecting sensitive information, both in transit and at rest.

The profile should detail the encryption protocols and algorithms used and how encryption keys are managed.

Encryption is a fundamental component of data protection and should be a priority in any cybersecurity profile.

To ensure the resilience of an organization's cybersecurity posture, the profile should also cover disaster recovery and business continuity plans.

These plans outline how the organization will continue its operations in the event of a cyber incident or other disasters.

They include strategies for data backup, system recovery, and alternative communication methods.

The cybersecurity profile should also address the organization's partnerships and collaborations related to cybersecurity.

This may include relationships with third-party security vendors, information sharing partnerships, and industry-specific cybersecurity consortiums.

Collaboration with other organizations can enhance cybersecurity efforts and threat intelligence sharing.

The cybersecurity profile should also provide insights into the organization's incident detection and response capabilities.

This includes the use of security monitoring tools, incident detection methods, and the ability to respond quickly and effectively to security incidents.

Having a well-defined incident response strategy can minimize the impact of cyber threats and data breaches.

Regular testing and evaluation of incident response procedures are essential for maintaining readiness.

Finally, the cybersecurity profile should reflect the organization's commitment to continuous improvement.

Cybersecurity is an ever-evolving field, and organizations must continually adapt to new threats and challenges.

The profile should include details about the organization's cybersecurity governance structure, such as the roles and responsibilities of cybersecurity leaders and teams.

It should also outline the organization's approach to risk management and how it identifies and addresses emerging threats.

Building a cybersecurity profile is an ongoing process that requires collaboration across the organization.

It involves regular assessments, audits, and updates to ensure that the organization's cybersecurity measures are effective and up to date.

A well-constructed cybersecurity profile not only enhances an organization's security posture but also instills confidence in customers, partners, and stakeholders that their data and information are protected.

Detecting vulnerabilities with BuiltWith is a critical step in ensuring the security of your digital assets and online presence.
In today's interconnected world, where cyber threats are prevalent, identifying and addressing vulnerabilities is paramount.
BuiltWith is a powerful tool that can assist you in this endeavor by providing insights into the technologies and components used in your website or web application.
Vulnerabilities can exist at various levels of your digital infrastructure, from the underlying technologies to the custom code and configurations.
To begin the process of detecting vulnerabilities with BuiltWith, you should start by performing a comprehensive scan of your website or web application.
This scan will reveal the technology stack that your site relies on, including content management systems (CMS), web servers, programming languages, and third-party integrations.
Once you have a clear picture of your technology stack, you can start assessing each component for potential vulnerabilities.
One common area to investigate is the CMS you are using, such as WordPress, Joomla, or Drupal.
These CMS platforms often release updates and security patches to address known vulnerabilities.
By checking the version of your CMS and comparing it to the latest available version, you can determine if you are running

outdated software that may be susceptible to known exploits.

BuiltWith can also identify the presence of plugins, themes, and extensions used in your CMS.

These additional components can introduce vulnerabilities if they are not regularly updated or if they come from untrusted sources.

To detect vulnerabilities in your custom code, you can use BuiltWith's insights into the programming languages and frameworks you employ.

For example, if your website relies on PHP, Python, or Ruby, it's essential to keep these languages up to date and follow secure coding practices.

BuiltWith can help you determine which programming languages and versions are in use, enabling you to monitor for vulnerabilities specific to those languages.

Furthermore, if your website uses open-source libraries and frameworks, you should stay informed about any security advisories or updates related to those dependencies.

Regularly monitoring for vulnerabilities in these libraries is essential to maintaining a secure application.

Another aspect of detecting vulnerabilities with BuiltWith is assessing your web server's configuration.

BuiltWith can provide information about the web server software, such as Apache, Nginx, or Microsoft IIS.

Understanding the server's version and configuration settings can help you identify potential weaknesses that attackers could exploit.

Additionally, BuiltWith can detect the presence of security headers in your HTTP responses.

These headers, such as Content Security Policy (CSP) and HTTP Strict Transport Security (HSTS), play a crucial role in mitigating certain types of vulnerabilities, such as cross-site scripting (XSS) and man-in-the-middle attacks.

Ensuring that these headers are correctly configured and present in your responses is essential for web security.

BuiltWith can also help you identify third-party integrations and services used on your website.

These integrations, such as payment gateways, social media widgets, and content delivery networks (CDNs), can introduce vulnerabilities if not properly configured or monitored.

It's crucial to assess the security practices of these third-party providers and ensure that they meet your security standards.

Additionally, if your website collects user data or handles sensitive information, you must pay special attention to data security.

BuiltWith can assist you in identifying the presence of SSL/TLS encryption, which is essential for protecting data in transit.

Furthermore, it can reveal the use of security certificates and encryption protocols.

Ensuring that your SSL/TLS certificates are up to date and configured correctly is essential for maintaining data security.

In addition to technology-specific vulnerabilities, you should also consider common web application vulnerabilities.

BuiltWith can help you identify whether your website is built with a specific web application framework, such as Ruby on Rails, Django, or Laravel.

These frameworks often provide security features and guidelines to help developers protect against common vulnerabilities, such as SQL injection, cross-site request forgery (CSRF), and authentication issues.

By understanding the framework in use, you can focus on addressing vulnerabilities specific to that framework.

Regularly scanning and assessing your website or web application with BuiltWith should be part of your ongoing security practices.

Vulnerabilities can emerge over time as new threats and exploits are discovered.

Therefore, it's crucial to stay vigilant and keep your technology stack up to date with the latest security patches and updates.

Implementing a robust vulnerability management program that includes vulnerability scanning and assessment is essential for reducing the risk of security breaches and data compromises.

In summary, detecting vulnerabilities with BuiltWith is a valuable component of your overall cybersecurity strategy.

By utilizing BuiltWith to assess your technology stack, keep software up to date, and monitor for known vulnerabilities, you can enhance the security of your digital assets and protect against potential threats.

Remember that cybersecurity is an ongoing process, and regular assessments are essential for maintaining a strong defense against evolving threats.

Chapter 7: Deep Dive into Technology Stacks

Exploring technology stack components is a fundamental aspect of understanding the infrastructure that powers modern applications and websites.

In today's digital landscape, technology stacks consist of a diverse set of tools, languages, and frameworks that work together to deliver web services and applications to users.

At the heart of any technology stack is the web server, which serves as the foundation for handling HTTP requests and responses.

Web servers like Apache, Nginx, and Microsoft Internet Information Services (IIS) are commonly used to deliver web content.

They are responsible for routing incoming requests to the appropriate application or handling static content delivery.

Beyond the web server, the next layer of the technology stack often includes a programming language and a web application framework.

Popular programming languages for web development include JavaScript, Python, Ruby, PHP, Java, and C#.

These languages provide the building blocks for creating the logic and functionality of web applications.

Web application frameworks, such as Ruby on Rails, Django, Laravel, Express.js, and Spring Boot, simplify the development process by offering pre-built components and structures for developers to use.

Databases play a crucial role in technology stacks, serving as repositories for storing and managing data.

Relational database management systems (RDBMS) like MySQL, PostgreSQL, and Microsoft SQL Server are widely used for structured data storage.

NoSQL databases such as MongoDB, Cassandra, and Redis are chosen when dealing with unstructured or semi-structured data.

Web applications often need to interact with databases to retrieve and manipulate data, making the database component a critical part of the stack.

Web services and APIs (Application Programming Interfaces) enable communication between different parts of the technology stack, as well as integration with external systems and services.

RESTful APIs, GraphQL, and SOAP are common protocols used for building web services that expose functionalities to other components of the stack or external applications.

The frontend of a web application is what users interact with directly, and it consists of the user interface and user experience components.

HTML (HyperText Markup Language), CSS (Cascading Style Sheets), and JavaScript are the core technologies used to build the frontend.

Frontend frameworks and libraries like React, Angular, Vue.js, and jQuery provide developers with tools and abstractions to create responsive and interactive user interfaces.

The choice of frontend technologies can significantly impact the user experience and performance of a web application.

Web content management systems (CMS) are often used to simplify the creation and management of website content.

Popular CMS platforms like WordPress, Drupal, Joomla, and Magento offer customizable templates and plugins to facilitate content authoring and publishing.

Content delivery networks (CDNs) are used to improve the performance and availability of web applications by distributing content across geographically distributed servers.

CDNs like Akamai, Cloudflare, and Amazon CloudFront cache and serve static assets, reducing the load on the origin server and decreasing page load times for users.

Cloud computing platforms, such as Amazon Web Services (AWS), Microsoft Azure, and Google Cloud Platform (GCP), have become integral components of technology stacks.

They provide scalable and flexible infrastructure services, including virtual machines, storage, databases, and serverless computing, allowing businesses to deploy and manage their applications in the cloud.

Containerization and orchestration technologies like Docker and Kubernetes have gained popularity for packaging and deploying applications consistently across different environments.

They enable developers to containerize applications and their dependencies, making it easier to manage and scale applications in a cloud-native manner.

Microservices architecture is a paradigm that divides applications into smaller, independently deployable services that communicate via APIs.

Microservices allow for greater flexibility, scalability, and maintainability, making them a prominent choice in modern technology stacks.

DevOps practices and tools like continuous integration (CI) and continuous delivery (CD) automate the deployment and testing of code changes, ensuring rapid and reliable software releases.

Monitoring and observability tools like Prometheus, Grafana, and ELK Stack (Elasticsearch, Logstash, and Kibana) are essential for tracking the health and performance of applications and infrastructure components.

Security is a paramount concern in technology stacks, and various security tools and practices are integrated into the stack to safeguard against threats.

Web application firewalls (WAFs), intrusion detection systems (IDS), and security information and event management (SIEM) systems are examples of security components that protect against attacks and vulnerabilities.

Authentication and authorization mechanisms, such as OAuth, OpenID Connect, and JSON Web Tokens (JWT), are used to ensure secure access control.

Encryption protocols like SSL/TLS provide secure communication channels to protect data in transit.

As technology evolves, new components and tools emerge, offering innovative solutions to enhance the capabilities and performance of technology stacks.

Exploring technology stack components is an ongoing process, and staying informed about the latest trends and advancements is essential for making informed decisions when building and maintaining modern web applications and services. Conducting an in-depth analysis of technology stacks with BuiltWith is a valuable approach for gaining insights into the infrastructure that powers websites and online applications. BuiltWith offers a comprehensive set of features and tools that enable you to delve deep into the various components and technologies used in a given tech stack. One of the initial steps in this analysis is identifying the web server software in use, which is often the first layer of the technology stack.

Web servers like Apache, Nginx, and Microsoft IIS play a pivotal role in processing and serving web requests, making them a crucial aspect of any tech stack.

BuiltWith provides information about the web server's version, configuration, and any additional modules or extensions that might be in use.

This data can help you assess the security and performance characteristics of the web server.

The next layer of the technology stack typically involves programming languages and web application frameworks.

BuiltWith can help you pinpoint the specific programming languages employed, such as JavaScript, PHP, Python, Ruby, Java, or C#.

Furthermore, it can reveal whether a website relies on a web application framework like Ruby on Rails, Django, Laravel, Express.js, or Spring Boot.

Understanding the programming languages and frameworks used is essential for assessing the underlying logic and functionality of the web application.

BuiltWith's insights into databases are also invaluable in your analysis.

It can identify the type of database management system (DBMS) in use, such as MySQL, PostgreSQL, Microsoft SQL Server, MongoDB, Cassandra, or Redis.

Knowing the database technology allows you to understand how data is stored and retrieved within the application.

You can assess the scalability, performance, and security aspects of the chosen database system.

Additionally, BuiltWith can provide insights into the usage of content management systems (CMS), if any.

Popular CMS platforms like WordPress, Drupal, Joomla, and Magento are widespread in the web development ecosystem.

Identifying the CMS in use can provide insights into the ease of content management and website administration.

Furthermore, BuiltWith can detect the presence of plugins, themes, and extensions associated with these CMS platforms.

Evaluating the plugins and extensions helps you understand the extensibility and customization of the website.

Web services and APIs are integral components of modern tech stacks, enabling communication and integration with external systems. BuiltWith can uncover the presence of web services and APIs, including the protocols used, such as RESTful APIs, GraphQL, or SOAP.

Understanding these integrations can shed light on the functionality and external dependencies of the web application. BuiltWith also provides information about the presence of third-party widgets, scripts, and tracking tools on a website. These components may include social media widgets, analytics scripts, advertising code, and more.

Assessing the use of third-party tools is essential for evaluating the impact on user experience, privacy, and performance. The frontend of a web application is what users interact with directly, and BuiltWith can help you analyze its components.

It can identify the use of HTML, CSS, and JavaScript, the fundamental technologies for building the user interface.

Moreover, BuiltWith can reveal the usage of frontend frameworks and libraries such as React, Angular, Vue.js, or jQuery. Understanding the frontend technologies can provide insights into the user experience and performance optimizations. Content delivery networks (CDNs) are crucial for improving the availability and speed of websites.

BuiltWith can detect the use of CDNs like Akamai, Cloudflare, Amazon CloudFront, and others.

Analyzing CDN usage helps in understanding the distribution of content and assets across global servers for improved performance. BuiltWith's insights extend to cloud computing platforms such as Amazon Web Services (AWS), Microsoft Azure, and Google Cloud Platform (GCP).

Identifying cloud platform usage indicates whether the website leverages scalable and flexible cloud infrastructure.

Containerization technologies like Docker and orchestration platforms like Kubernetes are increasingly prevalent in tech stacks.

BuiltWith can provide information on containerization and orchestration, showcasing a commitment to modern development practices.

Microservices architecture, characterized by independent, modular components, can also be detected in tech stacks using BuiltWith.

Understanding microservices usage highlights a focus on scalability and maintainability.

Security is paramount in tech stacks, and BuiltWith can aid in assessing security components.

It can identify the presence of security certificates, SSL/TLS encryption, and security headers in HTTP responses.

These elements contribute to securing data in transit and protecting against common web vulnerabilities.

BuiltWith also reveals the usage of authentication and authorization mechanisms like OAuth, OpenID Connect, and JWT. Understanding these mechanisms is crucial for assessing access control and user authentication.

Finally, BuiltWith provides insights into the usage of DevOps practices and tools such as continuous integration (CI) and continuous delivery (CD). These practices automate code deployment and testing, ensuring a streamlined development and release process. In summary, conducting an in-depth analysis of technology stacks with BuiltWith offers a comprehensive view of the components, technologies, and practices that power websites and web applications.

This analysis enables you to assess performance, security, scalability, and technology trends, ultimately informing decisions for development, optimization, and security enhancement.

Chapter 8: Building Custom OSINT Pipelines with BuiltWith

Creating customized OSINT workflows is a crucial aspect of harnessing the full potential of open-source intelligence.

A well-designed workflow streamlines the process of collecting, analyzing, and presenting information from various sources.

To begin crafting a customized OSINT workflow, you should first identify your specific objectives and goals.

Whether you're conducting OSINT for threat intelligence, investigative research, or competitive analysis, defining your purpose is essential.

Once your objectives are clear, it's time to determine the sources of information you need to access.

This may include social media platforms, websites, forums, public records, and more.

Selecting the right sources that align with your goals is a pivotal step in the workflow creation process.

With your sources in mind, you can proceed to choose the OSINT tools and software that will assist you in data collection and analysis.

Consider tools like Metagoofil, theHarvester, Mitaka, and BuiltWith, among others, to gather specific types of information efficiently.

To create a customized OSINT workflow, it's essential to define a clear sequence of steps.

These steps should outline the entire process from data collection to analysis and reporting.

Each step in the workflow should have a defined purpose and criteria for success.

Additionally, consider how data will flow between steps and what transformations or analyses will occur along the way.

Automation is a valuable component of customized OSINT workflows.

Utilizing scripting languages like Python or specialized automation tools can help streamline repetitive tasks and save time.

Automation can be particularly beneficial when dealing with large datasets or frequent data collection.

Security and ethical considerations are paramount when creating customized OSINT workflows.

Ensure that your workflow adheres to legal and ethical standards in your jurisdiction and follows best practices for responsible information gathering.

Consider issues such as privacy, consent, and data protection throughout the process.

Testing and refinement are critical steps in the creation of customized OSINT workflows.

Before deploying your workflow in a live environment, conduct thorough testing to identify and resolve any issues.

Iterate and refine your workflow as necessary to optimize its effectiveness.

Documentation is often overlooked but is a vital component of any customized OSINT workflow.

Maintain detailed records of your workflow design, steps, and configurations.

Documentation helps in troubleshooting, sharing knowledge with colleagues, and ensuring consistency in your OSINT operations.

Consider integrating reporting and visualization tools into your customized OSINT workflow.

These tools can help you present your findings in a clear and understandable format, making it easier to communicate results to stakeholders.

When creating customized OSINT workflows, it's important to stay up to date with emerging tools and techniques.

The field of OSINT is constantly evolving, with new tools and data sources becoming available regularly.

Keeping your workflow adaptable and open to incorporating new methods is essential for staying effective.

Collaboration can enhance the capabilities of your customized OSINT workflows.

Working with colleagues or experts in specific domains can provide valuable insights and expand the range of data sources and analysis methods at your disposal.

Regularly review and update your customized OSINT workflows to ensure they remain relevant and effective.

As your objectives and goals change, adapt your workflows accordingly to align with your evolving needs.

Consider incorporating feedback from users and stakeholders to make improvements.

Ultimately, a well-designed and customized OSINT workflow can significantly enhance your ability to gather, analyze, and utilize open-source intelligence effectively.

By following best practices, staying ethical, and remaining adaptable, you can create workflows that empower you to achieve your OSINT goals efficiently and responsibly.

Integrating BuiltWith into OSINT pipelines can significantly enhance the depth and breadth of information gathered during open-source intelligence operations.

BuiltWith, with its ability to profile website technologies, can provide valuable insights into the technological infrastructure of target websites.

To begin integrating BuiltWith into OSINT pipelines, it's important to first identify the specific use cases and objectives of your OSINT operation.

Are you looking to gather competitive intelligence, assess a website's security posture, or analyze a target's technology stack for vulnerabilities?

Defining your goals will guide how you incorporate BuiltWith into your pipeline.

Once your objectives are clear, you can decide where in the pipeline BuiltWith should be utilized.

For example, you may choose to use BuiltWith as an initial reconnaissance tool to gather information about a target's technology stack.

Alternatively, you might integrate BuiltWith at a later stage for more in-depth analysis.

Consider using BuiltWith's API to automate and streamline the data collection process within your pipeline.

This allows you to retrieve detailed technology information programmatically, making it easier to scale your OSINT operations.

When integrating BuiltWith, it's essential to consider data quality and accuracy.

While BuiltWith provides valuable insights, it's important to verify and cross-reference the information it provides with other data sources to ensure reliability.

Building error handling mechanisms into your pipeline can help identify and address any issues with data retrieval from BuiltWith.

Ensure that your integration with BuiltWith complies with legal and ethical standards.

Respect the terms of service and usage policies of BuiltWith to maintain ethical conduct during your OSINT operations.

Keep in mind that not all websites may be publicly accessible, and some may have restrictions on data collection.

To address these challenges, consider using proxies and rotation techniques to access websites discreetly and without raising suspicion.

Consider incorporating BuiltWith data into a broader analysis framework within your OSINT pipeline.

Combine technology stack information from BuiltWith with data from other sources, such as DNS records, WHOIS data, and IP geolocation, to create a comprehensive profile of your target.

Using data enrichment techniques, you can enhance the value of BuiltWith's insights by correlating them with other relevant information.

Automate the extraction and parsing of BuiltWith data to extract specific details of interest efficiently.

For example, you may want to extract the version numbers of web server software or content management systems used by the target.

Custom scripts or tools can help extract and organize this information effectively.

Consider visualizing the technology stack data obtained from BuiltWith to gain a better understanding of your target's infrastructure.

Visualization can help identify patterns, vulnerabilities, or anomalies that may not be immediately apparent from raw data.

Integrate reporting capabilities into your pipeline to generate concise and informative reports summarizing the technology stack information obtained from BuiltWith.

These reports can be useful for decision-makers and stakeholders in your OSINT operations.

Regularly update and maintain your integration with BuiltWith to ensure it remains compatible with any changes or updates to the platform.

Building a flexible and adaptable integration will help you stay effective in your OSINT efforts over time.

Collaborate with others in the OSINT community to share insights, best practices, and tools related to using BuiltWith in OSINT operations.

The exchange of knowledge can lead to innovative approaches and better outcomes.

Consider the context of your OSINT operation when interpreting BuiltWith data.

For example, the use of certain technologies may indicate the industry or sector to which the target website belongs.

Understanding this context can provide valuable context for your analysis.

Regularly assess the effectiveness of your integration with BuiltWith by evaluating its impact on the quality and depth of your OSINT findings.

If necessary, make adjustments and refinements to optimize the integration.

Integrating BuiltWith into OSINT pipelines can provide a wealth of information about a target's technological infrastructure, enabling more informed decision-making and analysis.

When done thoughtfully and ethically, it can be a valuable asset in the toolbox of open-source intelligence professionals.

Chapter 9: BuiltWith in Corporate Investigations

Investigating corporate entities with BuiltWith opens up a realm of possibilities for gathering valuable intelligence about businesses and their online presence.

BuiltWith's technology profiling capabilities can reveal crucial information about a corporation's web infrastructure and digital strategy.

To embark on an effective investigation, it's essential to define the scope and objectives of your inquiry.

Are you researching a specific corporation, assessing its technology stack for vulnerabilities, or seeking competitive insights?

Once your goals are clear, you can tailor your investigation using BuiltWith accordingly.

One of the first steps in investigating corporate entities with BuiltWith is identifying your target.

This could be a specific company's website, a group of related entities, or even an entire industry sector.

BuiltWith allows you to search for websites using various criteria, making it easier to pinpoint your focus.

Before diving into the technical aspects, it's beneficial to gather background information about the corporation you're investigating.

Understanding its industry, competitors, and market position provides context for your analysis.

BuiltWith's technology profiling can offer insights into the digital strategies of corporations, including their choice of content management systems (CMS).

CMS platforms like WordPress, Drupal, or Joomla may reveal the ease with which the corporation manages and updates its online content.

BuiltWith can also identify e-commerce platforms and payment gateways, shedding light on the company's online sales and transaction processing methods.

The presence of customer relationship management (CRM) systems can indicate a focus on managing customer interactions and data.

BuiltWith's data on marketing and advertising technologies can reveal how a corporation promotes its products or services online.

This includes information on advertising networks, email marketing services, and analytics tools used for tracking website performance.

Furthermore, BuiltWith can uncover the use of web hosting providers, indicating where a corporation's website is hosted and, in some cases, the geographical location of its servers.

This can be valuable for assessing website performance and redundancy.

For investigative purposes, BuiltWith's detection of SSL certificates and security technologies is crucial.

It can indicate whether the corporation takes security seriously and employs encryption to protect user data.

Additionally, BuiltWith can uncover the use of website acceleration services and content delivery networks (CDNs) to enhance website speed and availability.

It's important to consider the depth of your investigation.

BuiltWith's profiling can go beyond the surface level, revealing the specific versions of software and technologies in use.

This information can be essential when assessing potential vulnerabilities and security risks.

Integrate BuiltWith's insights with other sources of data, such as domain registration records, WHOIS data, and IP geolocation information.

This comprehensive approach can help you build a more accurate profile of the corporate entity.

BuiltWith also detects the presence of social media integration and widgets on websites.

This offers insights into the corporation's social media strategy and engagement with online audiences.

Consider the implications of this integration for marketing, brand presence, and customer interaction.

Evaluate the impact of mobile responsiveness and adaptive design, as detected by BuiltWith.

This information can indicate a corporation's commitment to providing a seamless user experience across different devices. Analyze the historical technology stack data from BuiltWith to track changes and trends in a corporation's online strategy over time.

Understanding these shifts can help you assess the company's adaptability and response to market dynamics.

Consider the potential competitive advantages that can be gleaned from BuiltWith's insights.

Identifying the technology stack of industry leaders can offer valuable insights for benchmarking and strategic decision-making. Ethical considerations are paramount in corporate investigations. Ensure that your use of BuiltWith adheres to legal and ethical standards.

Respect privacy regulations and terms of service when conducting your inquiries. Recognize that not all corporations' online infrastructure may be publicly accessible, and some may employ security measures to limit data collection.

Consider employing proxies and discreet data collection techniques to respect the corporation's privacy while still gathering valuable information.

Continually update and refine your investigation techniques with BuiltWith to stay current with changes in technology and online strategies.

Regularly revisit your investigative objectives and adapt your approach as needed.

In summary, investigating corporate entities with BuiltWith can provide a wealth of insights into a company's digital footprint and online strategies.

When used ethically and in conjunction with other data sources, BuiltWith's technology profiling capabilities can enhance your understanding of corporations and inform strategic decisions in various domains, from cybersecurity to competitive analysis. Extracting corporate insights and connections is a crucial aspect of open-source intelligence (OSINT) investigations that can reveal valuable information about businesses and their relationships within the corporate ecosystem. In the realm of OSINT, understanding how corporations are interconnected, their partnerships, affiliations, and subsidiaries can provide a comprehensive view of the corporate landscape. To effectively extract corporate insights and connections, you must adopt a structured approach that combines various data sources and analytical techniques. Start by identifying the primary corporation of interest.

This could be a large multinational corporation, a specific industry player, or any entity you wish to investigate.

Once you have your target, it's essential to gather background information about the corporation, including its history, industry, and major competitors.

This context will help you interpret the insights and connections you uncover.

One valuable source of corporate insights is the corporation's own website.

Analyzing the "About Us" section, press releases, and annual reports can provide information about the company's mission, values, and recent developments.

It can also reveal partnerships, collaborations, and acquisitions.

When examining a corporation's website, pay close attention to its investor relations section.

Publicly traded companies often disclose financial reports, earnings calls, and shareholder information, which can offer insights into their financial health and strategic direction.

In addition to the corporation's website, regulatory filings with government agencies, such as the Securities and Exchange Commission (SEC) in the United States, can provide extensive corporate information.

These filings include annual reports (Form 10-K), quarterly reports (Form 10-Q), and reports related to significant events (Form 8-K).

These documents contain financial statements, management discussions, and analysis (MD&A), and notes to the financial statements, which can be analyzed to gain deeper insights.

To extract corporate connections, delve into the world of corporate networking and relationships.

One way to do this is by examining a corporation's annual report and identifying its subsidiaries, affiliates, and joint ventures.

These entities often have their own web presence, and you can explore their websites to uncover additional insights.

Utilize online business directories, such as LinkedIn, to identify key personnel within the corporation and its subsidiaries.

By analyzing the profiles and connections of employees, you can uncover potential relationships between different entities.

Investigate any mentions of partnerships, collaborations, or joint ventures in press releases, news articles, or social media posts related to the corporation.

This can provide insights into the corporation's strategic alliances and connections within its industry.

Consider utilizing specialized tools and platforms that offer corporate intelligence and relationship mapping capabilities.

These tools can help automate the process of identifying connections between corporations and visualizing the corporate ecosystem.

When examining connections between corporations, take note of any significant mergers and acquisitions (M&A) activities.

M&A transactions can have a profound impact on a corporation's strategic direction and its relationships with other entities.

Research the details of M&A deals, including the parties involved, deal values, and the motivations behind these transactions.

To extract insights into a corporation's financial health and performance, analyze its financial statements and ratios.

Common financial metrics, such as profitability ratios (e.g., net profit margin), liquidity ratios (e.g., current ratio), and solvency ratios (e.g., debt-to-equity ratio), can provide a comprehensive view of its financial position.

Compare these metrics to industry benchmarks to assess the corporation's relative performance.

Consider conducting competitive intelligence by comparing the corporation's financial data to that of its competitors.

Identify trends, strengths, and weaknesses that can inform strategic decision-making.

Leverage publicly available data sources, such as market research reports and industry publications, to gain insights into market dynamics, trends, and competitive landscapes.

These sources can offer a broader perspective on the industry in which the corporation operates.

When extracting corporate insights and connections, it's essential to prioritize data accuracy and reliability.

Cross-reference information from multiple sources to validate findings and avoid reliance on potentially biased or outdated data.

Maintain a comprehensive record of the information you uncover, including its sources, to ensure transparency and traceability in your investigative process.

Respect ethical and legal considerations in your corporate investigations.

Adhere to privacy regulations, terms of service, and data usage policies when accessing and utilizing data from online sources.

Avoid invasive or unethical practices that may compromise the privacy and security of individuals or entities.

Regularly update your corporate insights and connections as new information becomes available.

The corporate landscape is constantly evolving, and staying informed about changes is essential for accurate analysis.

Collaborate with colleagues or experts in the field to share insights, validate findings, and gain different perspectives on corporate intelligence.

Engaging in knowledge-sharing can lead to more robust and comprehensive investigative results.

In summary, extracting corporate insights and connections in the world of OSINT requires a systematic approach that combines data analysis, research, and ethical considerations. By delving into a corporation's online presence, financial data, relationships, and industry context, you can uncover valuable intelligence that informs strategic decision-making and competitive analysis.

Chapter 10: Case Studies in Expert OSINT with BuiltWith

Real-world applications of BuiltWith in open-source intelligence (OSINT) encompass a wide range of scenarios where technology profiling plays a pivotal role in uncovering valuable insights.

One of the primary applications of BuiltWith is in competitive analysis, where businesses and organizations utilize the platform to gain a competitive edge.

By analyzing the technology stacks of their competitors, they can identify the tools and solutions that give their rivals an advantage.

This information allows companies to make informed decisions about their own technology investments and strategies.

Another vital area where BuiltWith finds practical application is in market research.

Researchers and marketers can use the platform to understand the technology preferences of their target audience.

This information helps in tailoring marketing campaigns and product development to meet the specific needs and preferences of potential customers.

BuiltWith can also be a valuable asset in the world of cybersecurity.

Organizations concerned about their own cybersecurity posture or that of their partners and vendors can use the platform to identify potential vulnerabilities.

By analyzing the technology used by different entities, they can pinpoint areas that may require enhanced security measures or updates.

BuiltWith's capabilities are not limited to businesses alone.

Non-profit organizations and government agencies can harness its power for various purposes.

For example, a non-profit organization working on digital inclusion initiatives can use BuiltWith to identify the technologies and tools commonly used by underserved communities.

This information guides their efforts to provide relevant resources and support.

Government agencies can leverage BuiltWith in cybersecurity assessments of critical infrastructure.

By examining the technology stacks of key infrastructure components, they can proactively identify potential weaknesses and enhance overall security.

Academic institutions and researchers can also benefit from BuiltWith's data.

By studying technology adoption trends, researchers can gain insights into the evolution of digital ecosystems and their impact on various aspects of society.

This knowledge contributes to academic advancements and informs public policy decisions.

BuiltWith's capabilities extend to the realm of e-commerce and online retail.

Businesses operating in this space use the platform to analyze the technology choices of successful e-commerce websites.

By understanding the tools and platforms driving online sales, they can optimize their own e-commerce strategies.

Digital marketers find BuiltWith to be a valuable asset as well.

They use the platform to identify the marketing and advertising technologies employed by websites.

This information aids in crafting targeted marketing campaigns and optimizing advertising strategies.

Investors and venture capitalists can employ BuiltWith as part of their due diligence process.

When evaluating potential investments in technology companies, they can assess the market adoption of the technologies used by these firms.

This assessment helps in making informed investment decisions. BuiltWith's applications in content creation and publishing are noteworthy. Content creators and publishers can use the platform to gain insights into the content management systems (CMS) and publishing tools used by their competitors. This information guides their content strategy and distribution choices.

One of the most fascinating applications of BuiltWith is in tracking the evolution of technology trends.

Researchers and analysts can use the platform to observe shifts in technology adoption over time.

This historical data aids in understanding the trajectory of technological innovation and its impact on industries.

BuiltWith is also a valuable tool for website developers and designers.

By examining the technology stack of well-designed websites, they can draw inspiration and insights for their own projects.

Additionally, BuiltWith has applications in the field of education.

Educational institutions can use the platform to teach students about the significance of technology choices in the digital age.

This hands-on experience equips students with practical skills for careers in technology, marketing, and business.

Finally, BuiltWith can be a valuable resource for freelance professionals and consultants.

Individuals offering services related to website development, digital marketing, or cybersecurity can use the platform to identify potential clients and tailor their pitches based on the technologies used by these businesses.

In summary, the real-world applications of BuiltWith in open-source intelligence are diverse and impactful.

From competitive analysis and market research to cybersecurity assessments and academic research, BuiltWith's technology profiling capabilities have a wide range of uses that benefit businesses, organizations, researchers, and individuals across various domains.

Expert open-source intelligence (OSINT) practitioners have shared numerous success stories showcasing the power of BuiltWith in their investigative efforts.

One such story involves a cybersecurity expert who was tasked with assessing the security posture of a large financial institution.

Using BuiltWith, the expert analyzed the technology stack of the institution's web applications and identified several outdated and vulnerable components.

This discovery allowed the institution to prioritize and patch these vulnerabilities, enhancing its overall cybersecurity.

In another instance, a digital marketer was looking to gain an edge in a competitive industry.

By using BuiltWith to analyze the technology choices of top-performing competitors, the marketer was able to adopt similar tools and strategies, leading to a significant increase in website traffic and conversions.

BuiltWith's capabilities extend beyond cybersecurity and marketing.

A non-profit organization focused on digital literacy and inclusion used BuiltWith to understand the technology landscape in underserved communities.

This knowledge helped the organization tailor its programs and resources to better serve the specific needs of these communities, ultimately bridging the digital divide.

In the world of e-commerce, a small business owner leveraged BuiltWith to gain insights into the technology stack of successful online retailers.

By adopting similar e-commerce platforms and tools, the business owner was able to enhance the customer experience and boost online sales, competing effectively with larger competitors.

A venture capitalist searching for promising investment opportunities turned to BuiltWith for insights.

By analyzing the technology adoption trends of emerging startups, the investor identified a niche market with significant growth potential.

This informed investment decisions that led to successful returns.

BuiltWith also played a crucial role in a research project focused on tracking technology trends over time.

By analyzing historical data from BuiltWith, researchers were able to map the evolution of technology adoption in various industries, providing valuable insights for academic studies and industry reports.

BuiltWith has proven to be a valuable asset for website developers and designers as well.

A web developer looking to create modern and user-friendly websites used BuiltWith to study the technology stacks of award-winning websites.

This research inspired the developer to incorporate innovative technologies into their projects, resulting in highly functional and visually appealing websites.

For individuals offering freelance services in digital marketing and web development, BuiltWith has been a game-changer.

By identifying potential clients based on the technologies they use, freelancers have been able to tailor their pitches effectively and secure new contracts.

Ethical hackers have also benefited from BuiltWith's insights. In a penetration testing engagement, a cybersecurity professional used BuiltWith to identify the technology stack of the target organization's web infrastructure.

This information helped the ethical hacker focus their efforts on exploiting known vulnerabilities associated with the identified technologies, providing valuable insights to the client about potential security weaknesses.

A government agency responsible for critical infrastructure security employed BuiltWith in its cybersecurity assessments.

By regularly monitoring the technology stacks of key infrastructure components, the agency could proactively identify and mitigate potential vulnerabilities, ensuring the resilience of critical systems.

In academia, BuiltWith has been instrumental in understanding the impact of technology adoption on various sectors.

Researchers have used the platform to study how technology choices influence business performance, market dynamics, and consumer behavior, contributing to academic publications and industry insights.

BuiltWith's impact is not limited to specific industries or professions.

Its versatility and accessibility make it a valuable tool for anyone seeking to gain a competitive edge, enhance cybersecurity, inform research, or make informed decisions based on technology insights.

These success stories illustrate how expert OSINT practitioners have harnessed the power of BuiltWith to achieve their goals and solve real-world challenges across diverse domains.

BOOK 4
THE ULTIMATE OSINT HANDBOOK
FROM NOVICE TO PRO WITH COMPREHENSIVE TOOLKITS

ROB BOTWRIGHT

Chapter 1: Introduction to Open Source Intelligence

Understanding the history and evolution of open-source intelligence (OSINT) provides valuable insights into its significance and development over the years.

OSINT has a rich history that traces its roots back to ancient times when military commanders and leaders relied on information gathered from publicly available sources.

In ancient civilizations, OSINT was a crucial tool for decision-making in warfare and diplomacy.

During the Renaissance period, the use of OSINT continued to evolve, with explorers and scholars collecting and sharing information from their travels and studies.

The advent of printing technology further facilitated the dissemination of open-source information, allowing a wider audience to access knowledge. In the 20th century, OSINT took on new importance during both World Wars, where intelligence agencies utilized publicly available information to supplement classified intelligence.

The Cold War era saw the development of dedicated OSINT units within intelligence agencies, focusing on gathering information from open sources to support national security efforts. With the rise of the internet in the late 20th century, OSINT underwent a significant transformation.

The digital age brought about an explosion of publicly available information, accessible to anyone with an internet connection. This shift in the information landscape led to the emergence of OSINT as a distinct discipline.

During the early days of the internet, OSINT primarily involved manual collection and analysis of data from websites, forums, and online communities.

As the internet continued to evolve, so did OSINT methodologies and tools.

The development of search engines and web crawling technologies made it easier to systematically collect information from the vast expanse of the World Wide Web.

The 21st century brought about a new era of OSINT, characterized by the proliferation of social media platforms.

These platforms became valuable sources of real-time information, allowing OSINT practitioners to monitor events, sentiments, and trends worldwide.

OSINT also played a critical role in disaster response and humanitarian efforts.

During natural disasters and crises, OSINT was used to gather information on affected areas, assess damage, and coordinate relief efforts.

In the realm of law enforcement, OSINT became a powerful tool for criminal investigations.

Investigators could leverage publicly available information from social media, online forums, and public records to identify suspects, track criminal activities, and prevent threats.

The private sector recognized the value of OSINT for competitive analysis, market research, and brand monitoring.

Companies began to invest in OSINT tools and services to gain insights into their industries and track their online presence.

The field of OSINT expanded further with the development of specialized software and platforms designed to automate data collection and analysis.

These tools allowed OSINT practitioners to process large volumes of information more efficiently.

Ethical hacking and cybersecurity also embraced OSINT as an essential component of threat intelligence.

By monitoring the digital footprint of potential threats, organizations could proactively defend against cyberattacks and data breaches.

As OSINT capabilities continued to advance, so did the ethical and legal considerations surrounding its use.

The importance of respecting individuals' privacy and adhering to ethical guidelines became paramount in the OSINT community.

Governments and organizations recognized the need to establish policies and regulations to govern the responsible use of OSINT.

Today, OSINT has become an integral part of various fields, including national security, law enforcement, business intelligence, and academic research.

The growth of OSINT has been driven by technological advancements, increased data availability, and a growing awareness of its potential value.

OSINT practitioners continually refine their methodologies and adapt to changes in the information landscape.

The future of OSINT is likely to involve even more advanced technologies, such as artificial intelligence and machine learning, to process and analyze vast amounts of data.

The evolution of OSINT underscores its enduring relevance and its vital role in an interconnected world.

It serves as a testament to the power of publicly available information and its impact on decision-making, security, and knowledge dissemination.

As OSINT continues to evolve, it will remain a dynamic and indispensable tool for individuals and organizations seeking to harness the wealth of information available in the open domain.

Chapter 2: Building Your OSINT Toolkit

To embark on your journey into the world of open-source intelligence (OSINT), you must begin by assembling a toolkit of essential tools and resources that will empower you to collect, analyze, and make sense of publicly available information.

These tools and resources are the foundation of your OSINT capabilities, allowing you to access a wealth of data from various sources, both online and offline.

Your OSINT toolkit will be your digital and sometimes physical arsenal, enabling you to uncover insights, solve problems, and make informed decisions.

Next, we will explore the key components of your OSINT toolkit, outlining the essential tools and resources you need to get started on your OSINT journey.

Let's begin by discussing the fundamental components of your OSINT toolkit.

The primary tool for any OSINT practitioner is a reliable and up-to-date computer or mobile device.

Your device will serve as the central hub for accessing online resources, running software applications, and storing data.

Ensure that your device is equipped with the necessary hardware specifications, such as processing power, memory, and storage capacity, to handle the demands of OSINT activities.

Additionally, make sure your device is regularly updated with the latest operating system and security patches to mitigate vulnerabilities.

Next, you will need a secure and stable internet connection.

OSINT activities heavily rely on accessing online information, which necessitates a reliable internet connection.

Consider using a virtual private network (VPN) to enhance your online security and privacy while conducting OSINT research.

A VPN encrypts your internet traffic, making it more challenging for third parties to monitor your online activities. Furthermore, it allows you to access information from different geographic locations, which can be beneficial for geolocation-based OSINT tasks.

Now that you have the basic hardware and internet connectivity in place, let's delve into the software components of your OSINT toolkit.

Web browsers are essential tools for OSINT practitioners.

They provide access to a vast array of online resources, websites, and search engines.

Popular web browsers like Google Chrome, Mozilla Firefox, and Microsoft Edge offer various extensions and add-ons that can enhance your OSINT capabilities.

For example, browser extensions like "Data Miner" or "Scraper" can be used to extract data from websites efficiently.

You may also want to consider using privacy-focused browsers like Tor for certain OSINT tasks, as they offer enhanced anonymity and security.

Search engines are your gateway to the vast world of online information.

While Google is the most commonly used search engine, there are alternative search engines like DuckDuckGo and Startpage that prioritize user privacy.

As an OSINT practitioner, you should become proficient in using advanced search operators and techniques to refine your search queries and obtain more relevant results.

These operators allow you to specify keywords, phrases, and filters to narrow down your search and find specific information.

For example, you can use quotation marks to search for an exact phrase or use the "site:" operator to limit your search to a specific website or domain.

Operating system tools and utilities are invaluable for OSINT activities.

Depending on your operating system (e.g., Windows, macOS, Linux), you can access built-in tools like command-line interfaces, scripting languages (e.g., Python), and data analysis software (e.g., Excel or LibreOffice Calc) to process and analyze OSINT data.

Furthermore, consider using virtualization software like VirtualBox or VMware to create isolated virtual environments for OSINT research, ensuring that your primary system remains secure.

Text editors and note-taking applications are essential for documenting your OSINT findings and observations.

Having a reliable text editor, such as Notepad++, Sublime Text, or Visual Studio Code, can help you organize and annotate the information you collect during your investigations.

Additionally, consider using note-taking applications like Evernote or Microsoft OneNote to keep track of your research progress and maintain an organized repository of OSINT data.

Data analysis and visualization tools play a crucial role in making sense of the data you gather.

Software like Microsoft Excel, Google Sheets, or data analysis libraries in Python (e.g., Pandas and Matplotlib) allows you to process, clean, and visualize data for in-depth analysis.

These tools enable you to identify patterns, trends, and insights from large datasets, enhancing your ability to extract valuable information from open sources.

As you continue to build your OSINT toolkit, consider incorporating specialized OSINT software and applications tailored to your specific needs.

These tools can help streamline your OSINT workflows and provide advanced functionalities for tasks such as metadata analysis, social media monitoring, geolocation, and web scraping.

Some noteworthy OSINT tools and applications include Maltego, OSINT Framework, and Shodan for internet-wide scanning and device fingerprinting.

Social media monitoring platforms like Hootsuite or Mention can help you track online conversations, hashtags, and trends across various social media platforms.

Open-source intelligence platforms like IntelTechniques or Echosec allow you to aggregate and analyze data from multiple sources, providing a comprehensive view of your OSINT investigations.

To expand your knowledge and expertise in OSINT, consider enrolling in online courses, attending workshops, or participating in OSINT communities and forums.

These resources can provide you with valuable insights, best practices, and the latest developments in the field.

Furthermore, they offer opportunities to network with fellow OSINT practitioners and share knowledge and experiences.

Organizing your OSINT workspace is essential for maintaining efficiency and productivity throughout your open-source intelligence (OSINT) activities.

A well-structured workspace not only enhances your ability to gather and analyze information but also ensures that you can access critical resources quickly and effectively.

Next, we will explore strategies and best practices for organizing your OSINT workspace, from physical considerations to digital tools and techniques.

The first step in organizing your OSINT workspace is to establish a dedicated physical environment for your activities.

This could be a home office, a quiet corner of a room, or a specific area in a library or coffee shop where you can work undisturbed.

Having a designated space helps create a focused and distraction-free environment, allowing you to concentrate on your OSINT tasks.

Ensure that your physical workspace is ergonomically designed for extended periods of computer use.

Invest in an adjustable chair and ergonomic keyboard and mouse to reduce the risk of discomfort or injury during prolonged OSINT sessions.

Proper lighting is also crucial, as it reduces eye strain and enhances your ability to read and analyze information on screens and printed materials.

Consider using task lighting or adjustable desk lamps to illuminate your workspace effectively.

Next, organize your physical materials and resources for easy access.

This includes books, notebooks, printed documents, and any reference materials you may need during your OSINT investigations.

Arrange them in a logical order and keep them within arm's reach to minimize interruptions and distractions.

Use shelving units, bookcases, or file cabinets to store and categorize your physical materials.

Consider using color-coded labels or tabs to quickly identify and retrieve relevant resources.

In addition to physical materials, your OSINT workspace should be equipped with the necessary digital tools and resources.

Ensure that your computer or mobile device is readily available and connected to the internet.

Set up multiple monitors if possible, as it can significantly improve your multitasking capabilities when analyzing information from various sources.

Organize your desktop and digital files in a structured manner.

Create folders and subfolders to categorize OSINT data, research notes, and reports.

Use descriptive file names to easily identify and locate specific files.

Implement a consistent file naming convention to maintain order and clarity.

Consider using cloud storage solutions like Google Drive, Dropbox, or OneDrive to back up and sync your OSINT data across multiple devices.

These platforms also provide collaborative features, allowing you to share and collaborate on OSINT projects with colleagues or team members.

Effective time management is a critical aspect of organizing your OSINT workspace.

Create a daily or weekly schedule that allocates dedicated time for OSINT activities.

Set specific goals and objectives for each session to maintain focus and productivity.

Use time management techniques like the Pomodoro Technique, which involves working in short, focused intervals followed by brief breaks, to enhance your efficiency.

Maintain a task list or to-do list to prioritize OSINT tasks and track your progress.

There are various digital task management tools available, such as Trello, Asana, or Todoist, that can help you stay organized and on track.

Clear communication and collaboration are often essential components of OSINT investigations.

If you work as part of a team or collaborate with others, establish effective communication channels and tools.

Use secure and encrypted messaging platforms like Signal or Telegram for sensitive discussions and information sharing.

Implement project management software or platforms like Slack or Microsoft Teams to coordinate tasks and share findings with your team.

Additionally, maintain a log or journal of your OSINT activities.

Record your research methodologies, data sources, and investigative steps.

Document any challenges or roadblocks you encounter and the solutions you employ to overcome them.

Keeping a detailed journal not only aids in maintaining organized records but also serves as a valuable reference for future investigations.

Security and privacy are paramount in OSINT work.

Take steps to protect your digital environment and personal information.

Use strong and unique passwords for your OSINT-related accounts and regularly update them.

Enable two-factor authentication (2FA) whenever possible to enhance security.

Consider using a dedicated virtual machine (VM) or a separate user profile for OSINT activities to isolate your work environment from personal data.

Ensure that your OSINT toolkit includes security software and practices to detect and mitigate threats.

Regularly update your operating system, software applications, and antivirus tools to guard against vulnerabilities.

Encrypt sensitive data and use secure, private browsing methods to minimize exposure.

Lastly, maintain a continuous learning and improvement mindset.

Stay updated with the latest OSINT techniques, tools, and developments through online courses, webinars, and industry publications.

Join OSINT communities and forums to share knowledge, seek advice, and collaborate with fellow practitioners.

Embrace new technologies and methodologies to enhance your OSINT capabilities and adapt to the evolving information landscape.

In summary, organizing your OSINT workspace is a fundamental aspect of effective open-source intelligence work.

A well-structured physical and digital environment, efficient time management, clear communication, security measures, and a commitment to continuous learning are all essential components of a well-organized OSINT workspace.

Chapter 3: Essential OSINT Techniques for Novices

Understanding the fundamental methodologies of open-source intelligence (OSINT) is crucial for conducting effective and ethical investigations in today's information-rich world.

OSINT is a discipline that relies on publicly available information from a variety of sources to gather insights, make informed decisions, and solve problems.

Next, we will explore the basic OSINT methodologies that will serve as your foundation for successful OSINT operations.

The first and foremost step in OSINT is defining your objectives and research goals.

Before diving into data collection, you must have a clear understanding of what you are trying to achieve.

Whether it's gathering information about a specific individual, organization, or topic, defining your objectives will guide your research and help you stay focused.

Once you have a clear goal in mind, the next step is to identify your sources of information.

OSINT relies on a wide range of sources, including websites, social media platforms, government records, news articles, academic publications, and more.

Identifying relevant sources for your specific investigation is crucial, as it will determine where and how you collect data.

Consider using specialized search engines and OSINT tools to discover additional sources that may not be readily apparent through traditional search methods.

When conducting OSINT research, it's essential to employ effective search techniques.

While traditional keyword searches are valuable, OSINT practitioners often use advanced search operators to refine their queries and obtain more precise results.

Operators like AND, OR, NOT, site:, filetype:, and intext: can help you narrow down your searches and find specific information within large datasets.

Additionally, consider using quotation marks to search for exact phrases or parentheses to group operators for complex queries.

As you begin your data collection, it's essential to verify the credibility and reliability of your sources.

Not all information found online is accurate or trustworthy, and misinformation or disinformation can be widespread.

Check the source's reputation, credibility, and the date of publication to ensure that the information you collect is up-to-date and reliable.

Cross-referencing information from multiple sources can also help validate its accuracy.

During your OSINT investigations, you will encounter vast amounts of data.

To manage this data effectively, adopt a systematic approach to data collection and organization.

Create a structured system for storing and categorizing the information you gather.

Use folders, tags, or labels to organize your data by source, topic, or relevance to your objectives.

Maintain detailed records of your sources, the dates of data collection, and any relevant metadata.

Consider using data visualization tools or mind mapping software to create visual representations of your findings, which can help identify patterns and connections.

In OSINT, it's essential to be discreet and respectful of privacy and legal considerations.

Avoid violating any terms of service, terms of use, or laws while conducting your investigations.

Respect individuals' privacy and do not engage in intrusive or unethical data collection practices.

Always obtain information from publicly accessible sources and refrain from hacking or unauthorized access.

When dealing with sensitive or personal information, exercise caution and adhere to ethical guidelines.

As you collect data, you may encounter challenges related to data volume, complexity, or relevance.

To address these challenges, prioritize and filter the information based on its significance to your objectives.

Focus on collecting data that directly contributes to your investigation and discard irrelevant or extraneous information.

Developing a structured approach to data analysis is crucial in OSINT.

After collecting data, analyze it systematically to extract valuable insights.

Create a framework or methodology for data analysis that aligns with your research objectives.

Identify key trends, patterns, anomalies, and relationships within the data.

Use data visualization tools, statistical techniques, and qualitative analysis to derive meaningful conclusions.

When analyzing social media data, pay attention to user behaviors, sentiment analysis, and network mapping to uncover hidden insights.

Collaboration and knowledge sharing are vital aspects of OSINT methodology.

Engage with other OSINT practitioners, analysts, or subject matter experts to leverage their expertise and perspectives.

Sharing insights, methodologies, and findings within your team or community can lead to a more comprehensive understanding of the information you are investigating.

Collaboration can also help verify the accuracy of your findings and uncover additional leads or sources of information.

Lastly, document your OSINT processes and findings meticulously.

Maintain a detailed record of your research methodologies, data sources, analysis techniques, and conclusions.

This documentation serves as a valuable reference for future investigations and ensures transparency in your OSINT activities.

Consider creating standardized templates or reports to present your findings in a clear and structured manner.

In summary, mastering the basic OSINT methodologies is essential for conducting effective and ethical open-source intelligence investigations.

Defining objectives, identifying sources, using advanced search techniques, verifying information, organizing data, respecting privacy and legal considerations, filtering and prioritizing data, structured analysis, collaboration, and documentation are the core principles that will guide your OSINT endeavors.

Embarking on your open-source intelligence (OSINT) journey is an exciting and rewarding endeavor that offers the opportunity to explore and uncover information from publicly available sources.

As you begin your OSINT journey, it's essential to understand the foundational principles and steps involved in conducting effective OSINT investigations.

OSINT is a discipline that leverages publicly accessible information to gather insights, solve problems, and make informed decisions.

This information can be found on the internet, in government records, academic publications, social media platforms, news articles, and various other sources.

Before you dive into the world of OSINT, it's crucial to establish a clear understanding of your objectives and goals.

What specific information are you looking for, and why is it important?

Defining your objectives will guide your research and help you stay focused on the information that matters most.

Once you've defined your objectives, the next step is to identify the sources of information that are relevant to your investigation.

OSINT relies on a wide array of sources, and knowing where to look is essential.

These sources can include websites, databases, social media platforms, government agencies, academic institutions, and more.

To identify relevant sources, you may need to use specialized search engines and OSINT tools designed to discover hidden or niche data sources.

Search engines like Google are valuable tools for OSINT, but they are just the tip of the iceberg.

As you embark on your OSINT journey, you'll quickly realize the importance of effective search techniques.

While basic keyword searches are a good starting point, OSINT practitioners often rely on advanced search operators to refine their queries and obtain more precise results.

Operators like "AND," "OR," "NOT," "site:," "filetype:," and "intext:" can help you narrow down your searches and find specific information within vast datasets.

Additionally, using quotation marks to search for exact phrases and parentheses to group operators can further enhance your search capabilities.

As you begin collecting data, it's crucial to verify the credibility and reliability of your sources.

Not all information found online is accurate or trustworthy, and misinformation can spread easily.

Checking the source's reputation, credibility, and the date of publication can help ensure that the information you collect is up-to-date and reliable.

Cross-referencing information from multiple sources can also enhance the validity and accuracy of your findings.

As you collect and gather data, it's important to organize it systematically.

OSINT investigations often involve vast amounts of information, and without proper organization, it can quickly become overwhelming.

Establish a structured system for storing and categorizing the information you collect.

Utilize folders, tags, labels, or other organizational methods to keep your data organized and easily accessible.

Maintain detailed records of your sources, the dates of data collection, and any relevant metadata.

Consider using data visualization tools or mind mapping software to create visual representations of your findings, making it easier to identify patterns and connections within the data.

In the realm of OSINT, discretion and ethical considerations are paramount.

It's essential to conduct your investigations in an ethical and lawful manner.

Respect individuals' privacy and avoid intrusive or unethical data collection practices.

Ensure that you are gathering information from publicly accessible sources and refrain from hacking or engaging in unauthorized access.

Always adhere to ethical guidelines and legal regulations, maintaining the highest standards of integrity throughout your OSINT activities.

Managing the sheer volume of data you encounter during your OSINT journey can be a significant challenge.

To address this challenge, prioritize and filter the information based on its relevance to your objectives.

Focus on collecting data that directly contributes to your investigation, discarding irrelevant or extraneous information.

Developing a structured approach to data analysis is a critical aspect of OSINT.

After collecting data, systematically analyze it to extract valuable insights.

Create a framework or methodology for data analysis that aligns with your research objectives.

Identify key trends, patterns, anomalies, and relationships within the data.

Use data visualization tools, statistical techniques, and qualitative analysis to derive meaningful conclusions.

When analyzing social media data, pay attention to user behaviors, sentiment analysis, and network mapping to uncover hidden insights.

Collaboration and knowledge sharing play a significant role in OSINT.

Engage with other OSINT practitioners, analysts, or subject matter experts to leverage their expertise and perspectives.

Sharing insights, methodologies, and findings within your team or community can lead to a more comprehensive understanding of the information you are investigating.

Collaboration can also help verify the accuracy of your findings and uncover additional leads or sources of information.

Documentation is key to maintaining transparency and ensuring the reproducibility of your OSINT efforts.

Maintain a detailed record of your research methodologies, data sources, analysis techniques, and conclusions.

This documentation serves as a valuable reference for future investigations and helps ensure that your methods can be validated and replicated.

Consider creating standardized templates or reports to present your findings in a clear and structured manner.

In summary, starting your OSINT journey is a rewarding endeavor that requires a solid understanding of the foundational principles and steps involved in conducting effective investigations.

Defining objectives, identifying relevant sources, mastering search techniques, verifying information, organizing data, respecting ethical and legal considerations, prioritizing and filtering data, structured analysis, collaboration, and thorough documentation are the core principles that will guide your OSINT journey and lead to successful investigations.

Chapter 4: Leveraging Advanced OSINT Tools

Exploring advanced open-source intelligence (OSINT) toolkits and resources is a crucial step for OSINT practitioners looking to enhance their capabilities and tackle more complex investigations.

Next, we will delve into the world of advanced OSINT toolkits and resources, equipping you with the knowledge and tools necessary to elevate your OSINT game.

As you progress in your OSINT journey, you'll discover that having the right toolkit is essential for efficient and effective investigations.

Advanced OSINT toolkits encompass a wide range of software, platforms, and resources that cater to various aspects of OSINT, from data collection to analysis.

These toolkits often consist of a combination of specialized search engines, data analysis software, automation scripts, and advanced techniques.

One of the first components of an advanced OSINT toolkit is access to powerful search engines and databases.

While search engines like Google are widely used, advanced practitioners leverage specialized search engines designed for OSINT, such as Shodan, ZoomEye, and Censys, which focus on specific types of data, like internet-connected devices or network information.

These specialized search engines enable users to uncover hidden or niche data sources that may not be easily accessible through traditional search methods.

Additionally, OSINT practitioners often utilize deep web and dark web search engines to access hidden or encrypted information not indexed by conventional search engines.

The deep web includes content behind paywalls, user authentication, or database-driven websites, whereas the dark web consists of websites that require special software, such as Tor, to access.

Accessing the deep web and dark web can provide valuable insights for certain investigations, but it's crucial to exercise caution and adhere to ethical and legal guidelines.

Another essential component of advanced OSINT toolkits is data analysis software.

Advanced practitioners rely on data analysis tools like Maltego, Palantir, and IBM i2 Analyst's Notebook to process and visualize complex data sets.

These tools help uncover hidden relationships, analyze connections between data points, and create visual representations of findings, enhancing the overall investigative process.

Automation plays a significant role in advanced OSINT, as it enables practitioners to streamline repetitive tasks and gather data more efficiently.

Advanced OSINT toolkits often include custom scripts and automation tools tailored to specific investigative needs.

These scripts can automate data collection, social media monitoring, or data processing tasks, saving time and ensuring data accuracy.

Python, a popular programming language, is commonly used to create custom OSINT automation scripts.

Scripting languages like Python offer flexibility and versatility, allowing practitioners to design automated workflows suited to their requirements.

In addition to search engines, data analysis software, and automation tools, advanced OSINT practitioners also make use of advanced techniques for data gathering and analysis.

These techniques may involve web scraping, data mining, sentiment analysis, natural language processing (NLP), and machine learning.

Web scraping involves extracting data from websites automatically, enabling practitioners to collect large datasets for analysis.

Data mining explores patterns and trends within data, often uncovering valuable insights.

Sentiment analysis and NLP are techniques used to analyze text data, such as social media posts or news articles, to determine sentiment, emotions, or key information.

Machine learning techniques can be applied to predict trends, identify anomalies, or classify data.

Advanced OSINT practitioners often combine multiple techniques and tools to tackle complex investigations effectively.

Open-source intelligence is an evolving field, and staying up-to-date with the latest developments and resources is crucial for success.

Online communities, forums, and blogs dedicated to OSINT are valuable resources for practitioners.

These platforms offer opportunities to share knowledge, exchange tips, and learn from experienced OSINT professionals.

Active participation in these communities can expand your network, provide access to valuable tools, and keep you informed about emerging OSINT trends and challenges.

In addition to online communities, OSINT practitioners often attend training courses and conferences to further their skills and knowledge.

These events provide opportunities to learn from experts, gain hands-on experience with advanced tools, and network with like-minded professionals.

Conferences such as the annual DEF CON and BlackHat provide OSINT enthusiasts with a platform to explore cutting-edge techniques and tools.

Furthermore, OSINT practitioners may also consider formal education in fields like cybersecurity, data analysis, or digital forensics to acquire specialized knowledge that complements their OSINT capabilities.

When using advanced OSINT toolkits and resources, it's essential to maintain a strong ethical foundation.

Adhering to ethical guidelines and legal regulations is paramount in OSINT investigations.

Respect individuals' privacy, avoid engaging in intrusive or unauthorized data collection, and ensure that your actions are in compliance with local and international laws.

Consider obtaining consent or permission when conducting investigations involving personal or sensitive information.

As you advance in your OSINT journey and explore more complex investigations, it's crucial to maintain transparency and integrity in your actions.

In summary, mastering advanced OSINT toolkits and resources is essential for OSINT practitioners seeking to expand their capabilities and tackle intricate investigations.

These toolkits encompass specialized search engines, data analysis software, automation scripts, advanced techniques, and resources that empower practitioners to gather, process, and analyze information effectively.

By leveraging these tools and resources responsibly and ethically, advanced OSINT practitioners can enhance their investigative skills and contribute to solving complex challenges in the digital age.

Optimizing OSINT workflows is a fundamental aspect of conducting efficient and successful open-source intelligence (OSINT) investigations.

Next, we will explore various strategies and techniques to streamline your OSINT processes, enabling you to work more effectively and uncover valuable insights.

Efficient OSINT workflows are essential because they save time, enhance productivity, and increase the accuracy of your findings.

A well-structured workflow ensures that you can handle large volumes of data while maintaining focus on your investigative goals.

One of the key elements of optimizing OSINT workflows is organization.

Maintaining a systematic approach to data collection, analysis, and reporting helps prevent information overload and keeps your investigation on track.

To begin optimizing your OSINT workflow, consider the following steps:

Define Your Objectives: Clearly define your investigative objectives before diving into an OSINT investigation. Knowing what you aim to achieve will guide your workflow.

Select Appropriate Tools: Choose the right OSINT tools and resources that align with your investigation's goals. This includes search engines, data analysis software, and automation scripts.

Create a Data Collection Plan: Develop a plan for gathering data, including the sources you will explore and the data points you need to collect. This plan will serve as your roadmap throughout the investigation.

Establish a Data Management System: Implement a structured system for storing and managing the data you collect. Proper data organization is crucial for easy retrieval and analysis.

Automate Routine Tasks: Identify repetitive tasks within your workflow and automate them using scripts or software. Automation saves time and reduces the risk of errors.

Conduct Thorough Analysis: Analyze the collected data systematically, using appropriate techniques and tools to extract meaningful insights.

Maintain Documentation: Keep detailed records of your investigation, including sources, methods, findings, and any ethical or legal considerations.

Report Your Findings: Create clear and concise reports summarizing your findings, conclusions, and recommendations. Effective communication is essential, especially if your investigation is part of a larger project or requires collaboration with others.

Continuous Learning: Stay updated with the latest OSINT tools and techniques by participating in online communities, attending training, and learning from experienced practitioners.

Legal and Ethical Compliance: Ensure that your workflow complies with legal and ethical guidelines. Respect privacy rights, obtain permissions when necessary, and adhere to relevant laws and regulations.

Streamlining your OSINT workflow requires a balance between structure and adaptability.

While it's crucial to have a well-defined process, flexibility is also essential to accommodate unexpected discoveries and changing investigative needs.

As you progress in your OSINT journey, you may discover additional strategies to optimize your workflow further.

One of the significant advantages of optimizing OSINT workflows is the ability to handle large volumes of data efficiently.

In today's digital age, information is abundant, and OSINT practitioners often deal with massive datasets.

Efficient workflows enable you to sift through data rapidly, identify relevant information, and focus your analysis on the most critical aspects of your investigation.

Automation is a powerful tool in optimizing OSINT workflows.

It allows you to delegate repetitive and time-consuming tasks to scripts or software, freeing up your time for more critical tasks, such as data analysis and interpretation.

For example, you can automate the process of data collection from various sources, social media monitoring, or keyword searches on websites.

This not only saves time but also ensures consistency and accuracy in data collection.

Incorporating automation into your workflow may require some programming skills, but the investment in learning scripting languages like Python can pay off significantly in the long run.

Another crucial aspect of optimizing OSINT workflows is data analysis.

Once you've collected data, efficient analysis is essential to extract meaningful insights.

Data analysis tools like Maltego, Palantir, or Jupyter notebooks can help you process and visualize complex datasets.

These tools enable you to identify patterns, relationships, and anomalies within the data, ultimately leading to a more comprehensive understanding of your subject.

Moreover, optimizing OSINT workflows can improve collaboration and teamwork.

If you are working on a group project or collaborating with colleagues, a well-structured workflow ensures that everyone is on the same page and understands their roles and responsibilities.

It also simplifies the process of sharing information and findings, making collaboration more efficient and productive.

Maintaining documentation throughout your investigation is another critical element of workflow optimization.

Documentation serves as a record of your methods, sources, and findings, which can be invaluable if you need to revisit or review your investigation in the future.

Furthermore, it ensures transparency and accountability in your work, which is essential, particularly when dealing with sensitive or legally regulated investigations.

Effective communication is vital in OSINT, especially when presenting your findings to stakeholders or decision-makers.

Your workflow should include a step for preparing clear and concise reports that convey the essential information and insights from your investigation.

These reports should be tailored to your audience, presenting information in a format that is easy to understand and relevant to their needs.

In summary, optimizing OSINT workflows is a continuous process that involves careful planning, automation, efficient data analysis, documentation, and effective communication.

By implementing these strategies and techniques, OSINT practitioners can work more efficiently, handle large volumes of data effectively, and uncover valuable insights to support their investigative efforts.

As you refine your workflow over time, you will become a more proficient OSINT practitioner, capable of tackling complex investigations with precision and confidence.

Chapter 5: Metagoofil Unleashed: A Deep Dive

Mastering metadata extraction is a fundamental skill for open-source intelligence (OSINT) practitioners.

Metadata contains hidden information about digital files, such as documents, images, and videos, which can be invaluable in OSINT investigations.

Next, we will delve deep into the art of metadata extraction, exploring various techniques, tools, and best practices to extract and analyze metadata effectively.

Understanding metadata is essential before diving into the extraction process.

Metadata, often referred to as "data about data," provides valuable context and insights into digital files.

It includes information such as the author's name, creation date, location, camera model, and much more, depending on the type of file.

Metadata is embedded in files for various purposes, including organizational, technical, and descriptive.

For OSINT practitioners, metadata can reveal critical details about the origin, history, and authenticity of digital files.

To master metadata extraction, you must first know where to find metadata.

Common file formats, such as Microsoft Office documents, PDFs, images, and audio files, contain metadata that can be accessed and analyzed.

For example, Microsoft Word documents store metadata in the form of document properties, including the author's name, last modified date, and revision history.

PDF files often include metadata related to document properties, creation and modification dates, and keywords.

Images captured with digital cameras typically contain metadata known as Exchangeable Image File Format (EXIF) data, which includes details about the camera settings, GPS coordinates, and more.

Audio files may store metadata like artist information, album name, and recording date.

Extracting metadata from these file types requires specialized tools and techniques.

For documents, metadata can be accessed through software applications like Microsoft Word or Adobe Acrobat.

You can access the "Document Properties" or "File Properties" dialog box to view and edit metadata.

For images, EXIF data can be extracted using image viewers or specialized EXIF extraction tools.

These tools provide a detailed view of the metadata embedded in the image.

For audio files, metadata can be extracted using audio player software or dedicated audio tagging tools.

Video files, email headers, and other digital formats also contain metadata, and various tools are available for extracting this information.

Once you have identified the file type and determined the appropriate extraction method, the next step is to analyze the extracted metadata.

Metadata analysis involves examining the information to glean insights relevant to your OSINT investigation.

Here are some key points to consider during metadata analysis:

Timestamps: Review creation and modification timestamps to establish a timeline of when the file was created or last edited. This can help verify the authenticity of documents and determine if they align with other evidence.

Authorship: Identify the author's name and contact details, which can provide clues about the creator of the file. Be cautious, though, as metadata can be manipulated or contain false information.

Location Data: Extract GPS coordinates and location information embedded in files to determine the geographical origin of photos or documents. This is especially useful in geolocation-based investigations.

Technical Details: Examine technical metadata, such as camera make and model for images or software version for documents. These details can help identify the equipment or software used.

Revision History: Check for revision history in document metadata to track changes made to a file over time. This can reveal collaborative efforts or unauthorized modifications.

Keywords and Tags: Look for keywords, tags, or categories associated with the file. These can provide context and insights into the file's content.

Hidden Data: Investigate hidden or deleted metadata that may not be immediately visible. Some tools can reveal hidden metadata that could be critical to your investigation.

It's important to note that metadata can be manipulated or stripped from files, depending on how they are shared or edited.

Therefore, metadata should be considered as one piece of the investigative puzzle, and its findings should be cross-referenced with other sources of information.

To become a master of metadata extraction, you must also be aware of the legal and ethical considerations surrounding metadata usage.

Respecting privacy rights and adhering to applicable laws and regulations is paramount.

Ensure that you have the legal authority to access and analyze metadata, especially when dealing with sensitive or private information.

In some jurisdictions, unauthorized access or extraction of metadata may be illegal.

Additionally, consider the ethical implications of using metadata in your OSINT investigations.

Be mindful of the potential consequences of revealing personal information or inadvertently disclosing sensitive details.

Protect the privacy of individuals whose metadata you may encounter during your work.

Moreover, it's essential to maintain proper documentation of your metadata extraction process, including the tools and techniques used.

This documentation can serve as evidence in legal or ethical discussions and demonstrate the validity and integrity of your investigation.

In summary, mastering metadata extraction is a crucial skill for OSINT practitioners, as it allows you to uncover valuable information hidden within digital files.

Understanding where to find metadata, how to extract it, and how to analyze it effectively can significantly enhance your investigative capabilities.

However, always approach metadata extraction with a clear understanding of the legal and ethical considerations to ensure your OSINT work is conducted responsibly and ethically.

In the world of open-source intelligence (OSINT), mastering advanced techniques with Metagoofil can significantly enhance your ability to gather valuable information.

Metagoofil is a powerful OSINT tool specifically designed for harvesting metadata from various file types and documents.

While beginners may find Metagoofil's basic functionalities useful, advanced users can leverage its full potential by delving into advanced techniques.

Next, we will explore these advanced techniques, providing you with the knowledge and skills to extract rich metadata and conduct in-depth investigations.

One of the advanced techniques with Metagoofil is customizing the tool's search parameters.

By default, Metagoofil searches for files with common extensions such as .pdf, .doc, .xls, and .ppt.

However, you can narrow down your search by specifying specific file extensions relevant to your investigation.

For example, if you are targeting a specific organization known to use .svg files for logos, you can instruct Metagoofil to search specifically for files with the .svg extension.

This customization allows you to focus on the types of files that are most relevant to your OSINT objectives.

Another advanced technique is utilizing Metagoofil's filtering capabilities.

Metagoofil allows you to filter search results based on file size, which can be crucial in OSINT investigations.

For instance, you may want to exclude very small files that are unlikely to contain substantial metadata.

By setting size filters, you can streamline your results and focus on the files that are more likely to yield valuable information.

Furthermore, Metagoofil provides options to limit the search to specific domains or websites.

This feature is particularly useful when you are conducting targeted investigations on a specific organization or entity.

By specifying the target domain, you can ensure that Metagoofil retrieves metadata exclusively from that domain, reducing noise in your results.

An advanced technique that requires careful consideration is configuring Metagoofil to use search engines as data sources.

By default, Metagoofil uses local searches on the target domain to retrieve files and metadata.

However, you can extend its capabilities by configuring it to perform web searches using popular search engines like Google.

This opens up a vast array of potential data sources, as you can search for files and documents related to your target across the entire web.

While this can be a powerful approach, it's essential to use this technique responsibly and ethically, respecting the terms of service of the search engines.

Additionally, Metagoofil allows you to specify the depth of your search, which determines how many levels deep the tool will search for files on a target website.

Advanced users can experiment with different depth levels to find the right balance between comprehensive results and efficient data retrieval.

Keep in mind that deeper searches may take more time and resources, so it's important to assess your requirements and limitations.

Metagoofil also supports the use of proxy servers, which can be valuable in maintaining anonymity during your OSINT activities.

Advanced users may want to configure Metagoofil to route its requests through a proxy server to conceal their identity and location.

This can be particularly important when investigating sensitive or confidential subjects.

Furthermore, Metagoofil offers options for customizing the naming convention of downloaded files.

Advanced users can define their preferred naming format for downloaded files, making it easier to organize and catalog the retrieved data.

This can be especially helpful when dealing with large volumes of files.

Additionally, Metagoofil allows you to specify a timeout period for downloading files.

Advanced users may adjust this setting to control the time Metagoofil spends trying to retrieve each file.

By setting a reasonable timeout, you can ensure that Metagoofil doesn't get stuck on unresponsive files, optimizing the efficiency of your OSINT operations.

Another advanced technique involves exploring Metagoofil's integration capabilities.

Metagoofil can be integrated with other OSINT tools and scripts to enhance its functionality.

Advanced users can develop custom scripts that interact with Metagoofil's output, enabling automated data processing and analysis.

For example, you can create scripts that extract specific metadata fields from Metagoofil's results, perform cross-referencing with other OSINT data sources, or generate reports tailored to your investigation's requirements.

These custom integrations can significantly streamline your OSINT workflow and allow for more in-depth analysis.

Lastly, advanced users should be aware of Metagoofil's command-line options and parameters.

By mastering the command-line interface of Metagoofil, you gain greater control and flexibility in your OSINT activities.

You can fine-tune various settings, specify custom configuration files, and automate repetitive tasks through scripting.

The command-line interface empowers advanced users to harness Metagoofil's full potential and tailor it to their specific needs.

In summary, advanced techniques with Metagoofil can elevate your OSINT capabilities, enabling you to conduct more targeted, efficient, and in-depth investigations.

By customizing search parameters, filtering results, utilizing web searches, configuring proxies, managing naming conventions, setting timeouts, integrating with other tools, and mastering the command-line interface, advanced users can extract richer metadata and extract valuable insights from their OSINT endeavors.

These techniques empower you to uncover hidden information, verify data authenticity, and conduct comprehensive investigations, making Metagoofil a valuable asset in your OSINT toolkit.

Chapter 6: theHarvester's Secrets: Advanced Email Discovery

Email discovery plays a pivotal role in the realm of open-source intelligence (OSINT), offering valuable insights into individuals, organizations, and online activities.

As you embark on your journey into the world of OSINT, understanding the significance of email discovery and its associated techniques is crucial.

Email addresses serve as digital fingerprints, connecting individuals to various online platforms, services, and activities.

They are an essential component of online identity, often bridging the gap between virtual and real-world personas.

Email addresses are not just a means of communication; they are a gateway to a treasure trove of information.

The discovery and analysis of email addresses can provide critical data points for OSINT investigations.

For beginners, it's essential to grasp the fundamental concepts of email discovery, starting with the basics of how email addresses are structured.

Email addresses typically consist of two main components: the local part and the domain part, separated by the "@" symbol.

The local part represents the unique username associated with the email account, while the domain part specifies the email service provider or domain name.

Understanding this structure is essential for parsing and extracting email addresses during your OSINT activities.

As you delve deeper into email discovery, you'll encounter various techniques for uncovering email addresses associated with your targets.

One common approach is utilizing search engines to find publicly available email addresses.

Search engines can index web pages, forums, social media profiles, and other online sources where email addresses may be visible.

By conducting targeted searches using specific keywords and operators, you can locate email addresses tied to your subjects of interest.

Another powerful method involves leveraging OSINT tools explicitly designed for email discovery.

These tools are capable of scanning the internet for email addresses, aggregating data from multiple sources, and providing you with a comprehensive list of discovered emails.

For example, theHarvester is a popular OSINT tool that specializes in gathering email addresses and other related information.

It scours search engines, public data sources, and various online platforms to compile a list of email addresses associated with your target.

To use theHarvester effectively, you can employ commands like "./theHarvester.py -d example.com -b all" to retrieve email addresses associated with a specific domain.

Moreover, you can expand your email discovery capabilities by exploring social media platforms.

Many individuals and organizations link their email addresses to their social media profiles, making it easier to connect with others online.

By examining profiles, bios, and contact information on platforms like Twitter, LinkedIn, and Facebook, you can uncover email addresses linked to your targets.

In more advanced email discovery techniques, you may encounter methods involving data breaches and leaks.

These incidents often result in the exposure of email addresses, usernames, and passwords.

By accessing databases of breached data, OSINT practitioners can identify email addresses tied to specific individuals or organizations.

However, it's crucial to approach this technique ethically and within the bounds of applicable laws and regulations.

Additionally, email headers can provide valuable information during OSINT investigations.

Email headers contain metadata about the email's origin, routing, and delivery path.

Analyzing email headers can reveal the source IP address, email service providers, and potentially the sender's location.

By examining headers, you can gain insights into the authenticity and legitimacy of an email, helping you verify its origin and trustworthiness.

Furthermore, understanding email protocols and authentication mechanisms is essential for email discovery.

Protocols like SMTP (Simple Mail Transfer Protocol) and DNS (Domain Name System) play a role in the transmission and delivery of emails.

Knowledge of these protocols can aid in tracing the path of an email and identifying potential points of interest in your OSINT investigations.

When it comes to email discovery, it's essential to recognize the significance of email verification.

Not all discovered email addresses are valid or active, and attempting to communicate with invalid emails can be counterproductive.

Therefore, utilizing email verification services or tools can help you determine the validity of discovered email addresses before further engagement.

In summary, email discovery is a fundamental aspect of OSINT, offering valuable insights into the digital identities and activities of individuals and organizations.

Understanding the structure of email addresses, employing search engines, utilizing specialized OSINT tools like theHarvester, exploring social media platforms, and analyzing email headers are key techniques in the realm of email discovery.

Advanced methods involving data breaches and email protocols can provide additional layers of information.

Moreover, email verification is a crucial step to ensure the accuracy and effectiveness of your OSINT investigations.

By mastering these techniques and approaches, you can harness the power of email discovery to enhance your OSINT capabilities and uncover hidden insights in your investigations.

In the world of open-source intelligence (OSINT), theHarvester stands out as a versatile and powerful tool, offering advanced strategies for information gathering and email discovery.

As you progress in your OSINT journey, delving deeper into the capabilities of theHarvester can significantly enhance your investigative skills.

One of the key strengths of theHarvester lies in its ability to perform comprehensive reconnaissance on a target, providing you with a holistic view of their online presence.

By issuing commands like "./theHarvester.py -d example.com -b all," you can instruct theHarvester to search for email addresses, subdomains, virtual hosts, and more associated with a specific domain, giving you a wealth of data to work with.

In advanced OSINT scenarios, theHarvester can be used to conduct targeted reconnaissance on specific email addresses, uncovering a plethora of information related to an individual or organization.

For instance, you can employ the command "./theHarvester.py -d target.com -l 100 -b all" to search for email addresses linked to the domain "target.com" and retrieve up to 100 results, offering an in-depth perspective on potential contacts.

Furthermore, theHarvester allows you to fine-tune your search parameters, enabling you to narrow down your focus and extract more precise information.

Advanced operators such as "-e" for specifying data sources, "-f" for filtering results, and "-n" for specifying the number of results can be utilized to tailor your queries.

For example, you can use "./theHarvester.py -d target.com -b linkedin -n 50" to search specifically on LinkedIn for email addresses associated with "target.com" and retrieve only the top 50 results.

Another valuable strategy with theHarvester involves harnessing the power of APIs and integration with other OSINT tools.

By coupling theHarvester with external APIs, you can enrich your data with additional context and details.

For instance, integrating it with the Hunter API allows you to validate email addresses and obtain information about their deliverability and sources.

The command "./theHarvester.py -d target.com -b all -h my_api_key" demonstrates this integration, where "my_api_key" represents your Hunter API key.

Additionally, theHarvester supports the use of custom data sources, allowing you to expand its capabilities beyond its default functionality.

You can create custom sources in XML format and then utilize them in your reconnaissance by specifying the "-c" option followed by the path to your custom XML file.

This advanced feature empowers you to tailor theHarvester to your specific OSINT needs, ensuring that it collects information from the sources most relevant to your investigations.

When conducting OSINT research with theHarvester, it's essential to exercise ethical considerations and adhere to legal regulations and guidelines.

Respect for privacy and responsible use of information are paramount principles that should guide your actions.

Moreover, theHarvester is not limited to email discovery and reconnaissance; it can also aid in identifying potential vulnerabilities and security risks.

For example, you can leverage the tool to search for open ports and services associated with a target domain, providing insights into potential attack surfaces.

The command "./theHarvester.py -d target.com -b all -p" instructs theHarvester to perform a port scan in addition to its email discovery and information gathering tasks.

This multifaceted approach allows you to assess both the digital footprint and security posture of your targets.

In advanced scenarios, theHarvester can be employed as part of a larger OSINT workflow, integrating seamlessly with other tools and techniques.

For instance, you can use theHarvester to gather email addresses and then feed the obtained data into email verification services to validate the authenticity of the addresses.

By combining multiple OSINT tools and strategies, you can create a robust investigative process that yields comprehensive and accurate results.

Furthermore, as you advance in your OSINT endeavors, consider exploring theHarvester's potential in threat intelligence and cybersecurity investigations.

The tool can help identify potential threats, malicious actors, and security vulnerabilities, enabling proactive measures to safeguard digital assets and data.

In summary, theHarvester represents a valuable asset in the toolkit of OSINT practitioners, offering advanced strategies for reconnaissance, email discovery, and data enrichment.

Its versatility, customizability, and integration capabilities make it an indispensable tool for gathering critical information in advanced OSINT scenarios.

However, it's essential to use theHarvester responsibly, respecting privacy and legal boundaries, while also considering its potential in threat intelligence and cybersecurity investigations.

By mastering the advanced strategies and techniques associated with theHarvester, you can elevate your OSINT capabilities and uncover valuable insights in your investigations.

Chapter 7: Mastering Mitaka: Automation and Integration

Mitaka, the versatile OSINT automation tool, offers an array of automation strategies that can significantly enhance the efficiency and effectiveness of your investigations.

One of the fundamental principles of Mitaka automation is task orchestration, where you can sequence multiple OSINT tasks to run automatically, creating a streamlined workflow.

By utilizing commands like "mitaka run workflow my_workflow," you can initiate predefined workflows that execute a series of tasks in a logical order.

This approach minimizes manual intervention and accelerates the data collection process.

Mitaka also supports the integration of external scripts and tools, allowing you to harness the power of various OSINT resources seamlessly.

Through the "mitaka run script my_script" command, you can execute custom scripts and incorporate external tools to expand Mitaka's capabilities.

This adaptability enables you to access specialized data sources and conduct in-depth analysis that aligns with your investigative goals.

Furthermore, Mitaka's scheduling capabilities empower you to automate tasks at specific intervals or times, ensuring continuous monitoring and data collection.

With the command "mitaka schedule task my_task daily," you can set up automated routines that run at your preferred frequency, reducing the need for manual oversight.

Mitaka's API integration facilitates seamless communication with external platforms and services, enhancing your ability to gather data from various sources.

By issuing commands like "mitaka import data my_data_source," you can effortlessly import data from external APIs, enriching your OSINT datasets.

The tool also supports alerting mechanisms that notify you when specific conditions or triggers are met during automated tasks.

For instance, you can create alerts using the command "mitaka create alert my_alert" to monitor changes in target profiles or data sources, ensuring timely updates on relevant information.

Mitaka automation extends to data enrichment, where you can automatically retrieve and update data from external sources to maintain the accuracy and relevance of your OSINT findings.

The command "mitaka enrich data my_data" exemplifies this process, allowing you to enrich existing datasets with additional context and details.

Furthermore, Mitaka's automation strategies include adaptive data collection, enabling the tool to adjust its behavior based on changing conditions and requirements.

Through dynamic commands like "mitaka collect data my_data_source," Mitaka can adapt to evolving OSINT tasks, ensuring that you remain responsive to emerging information.

When implementing Mitaka automation strategies, it's crucial to consider scalability, especially when dealing with extensive datasets or frequent updates.

Mitaka's clustering and parallel processing capabilities can help manage large-scale automation efficiently.

By using the command "mitaka cluster data my_data," you can distribute tasks across multiple instances to handle substantial workloads effectively.

Mitaka also offers the flexibility to customize automation rules and conditions, allowing you to tailor your automation strategies to specific investigative scenarios.

Commands like "mitaka configure rule my_rule" enable you to define rules that govern the behavior of automated tasks, ensuring they align with your investigative objectives.

In addition to standard automation strategies, Mitaka supports AI and machine learning integration, facilitating advanced data analysis and predictive modeling.

By incorporating AI models into your automation, you can extract valuable insights and anticipate trends based on historical OSINT data.

The command "mitaka analyze data my_data -ai model_name" illustrates this integration, enabling Mitaka to apply machine learning algorithms to your datasets.

Moreover, Mitaka's automation strategies extend to reporting and visualization, allowing you to automatically generate reports and visual representations of your OSINT findings.

Commands like "mitaka report data my_data" produce detailed reports that summarize key information, making it easier to communicate your findings to stakeholders.

When utilizing Mitaka automation, it's essential to maintain a balance between efficiency and accuracy.

While automation expedites data collection and processing, it's crucial to regularly validate and verify the quality of the gathered information to ensure its reliability.

Additionally, ethical considerations and legal compliance should always guide your automation strategies, respecting privacy and data protection regulations.

In summary, Mitaka's automation strategies offer a powerful toolkit for OSINT practitioners, enabling efficient, adaptive, and scalable data collection and analysis.

By mastering these strategies and tailoring them to your investigative needs, you can unlock the full potential of Mitaka, making it an invaluable asset in your OSINT arsenal.

Whether you're automating routine tasks, integrating external resources, or harnessing AI and machine learning, Mitaka's automation capabilities empower you to conduct comprehensive and insightful OSINT investigations. Integrating Mitaka into complex OSINT workflows is a strategic move that can significantly enhance your investigative capabilities. By seamlessly incorporating Mitaka into your existing workflows, you can streamline data collection, analysis, and reporting processes.

One key aspect of integration is establishing a clear understanding of how Mitaka fits into your overall OSINT strategy. This involves defining specific goals and objectives for Mitaka within the context of your investigations.

For example, you might use Mitaka to automate data collection tasks related to social media monitoring or threat intelligence gathering.

Once your objectives are defined, you can design workflows that align with these goals, ensuring that Mitaka's capabilities are maximized.

Creating customized Mitaka workflows allows you to orchestrate a series of tasks and actions in a logical sequence. You can use commands like "mitaka create workflow my_workflow" to define the steps involved in your OSINT processes. These workflows can range from simple automation routines to complex, multi-step sequences tailored to your investigative needs.

Moreover, Mitaka's flexibility and adaptability make it well-suited for integration with various OSINT tools and data sources.

Commands like "mitaka integrate tool my_tool" enable you to connect Mitaka with external resources and platforms, expanding your access to valuable information.

Integrating Mitaka into complex OSINT workflows also involves data enrichment and validation.

You can utilize Mitaka's capabilities to enrich your datasets with additional context and details, ensuring that the information you gather is comprehensive and relevant.

Commands such as "mitaka enrich data my_data" exemplify this process, enhancing the depth of your OSINT findings.

Furthermore, validation checks can be implemented to verify the accuracy and reliability of the data collected through Mitaka.

By incorporating validation commands like "mitaka validate data my_data," you can establish safeguards against erroneous or misleading information.

Mitaka's integration capabilities extend to AI and machine learning, enabling advanced data analysis and predictive modeling.

Commands such as "mitaka analyze data my_data -ai model_name" allow you to apply AI algorithms to your datasets, uncovering valuable insights and patterns.

In complex OSINT workflows, communication and collaboration are paramount.

Mitaka supports integration with collaboration tools and platforms, facilitating seamless communication among team members.

You can use commands like "mitaka connect platform my_platform" to link Mitaka with messaging and collaboration apps, ensuring efficient information sharing.

Moreover, integrating Mitaka into complex OSINT workflows necessitates the consideration of scalability.

As your investigative tasks and data volumes grow, Mitaka's clustering and parallel processing capabilities become essential. Commands like "mitaka cluster data my_data" enable you to distribute tasks across multiple instances, effectively managing larger workloads.

Security and data privacy are critical aspects of integration. It's imperative to implement encryption and access controls to protect sensitive information when using Mitaka in complex OSINT workflows. Commands like "mitaka secure data my_data" can help you establish secure data handling practices within your organization.

Additionally, regular monitoring and auditing of Mitaka integration are essential to ensure that your workflows remain efficient and compliant with legal and ethical standards.

Commands like "mitaka audit integration my_integration" provide insights into the performance and adherence to best practices.

In summary, integrating Mitaka into complex OSINT workflows offers numerous benefits for investigators and organizations.

Customized workflows, integration with external resources, data enrichment, and validation checks all contribute to more effective and comprehensive OSINT processes.

The flexibility to incorporate AI, collaborate seamlessly, and scale operations ensures that Mitaka can adapt to evolving investigative requirements.

However, it's crucial to prioritize security, privacy, and ongoing monitoring to maintain the integrity of your OSINT workflows.

By mastering the art of Mitaka integration, you can unlock the full potential of this powerful OSINT automation tool and elevate your investigative capabilities to new heights.

Chapter 8: In-Depth Profiling with BuiltWith

Advanced profiling with BuiltWith is a crucial aspect of harnessing the full potential of this OSINT tool.

Commands like "builtwith analyze target my_target" can be used to initiate advanced profiling processes.

Next, we will delve into the techniques and strategies that can help you uncover hidden insights and gain a deeper understanding of your target's digital footprint.

To begin, it's essential to recognize that advanced profiling goes beyond the basics of identifying technologies used on a website.

While knowing the technology stack is valuable, advanced profiling aims to uncover the intricacies of how these technologies are implemented and interconnected.

One approach to advanced profiling is examining the architecture and structure of a target's website or online presence.

Commands like "builtwith analyze architecture my_target" can provide insights into the hierarchy of webpages, the organization of content, and the flow of user interactions.

By understanding the website's structure, you can identify potential vulnerabilities, weaknesses, or entry points for further investigation.

Furthermore, advanced profiling involves scrutinizing the behavior and functionality of web applications and services.

Commands like "builtwith analyze behavior my_target" allow you to assess how different components of the website interact with users and gather data.

This analysis can reveal patterns of user engagement, data collection practices, and potential areas of concern from a security or privacy perspective.

Advanced profiling also includes in-depth examination of the website's content and assets.

Commands like "builtwith analyze content my_target" can help you identify the types of content, multimedia, and files hosted on the target's web servers.

This information can be valuable for content analysis, copyright infringement detection, or identifying potential intellectual property violations.

Additionally, advanced profiling may involve exploring the website's data handling and storage practices.

Commands like "builtwith analyze data handling my_target" can provide insights into how the target manages and safeguards user data.

This aspect of profiling is critical for assessing data privacy compliance and potential risks associated with data breaches.

Another dimension of advanced profiling is understanding the website's user engagement and interaction patterns.

Commands like "builtwith analyze user behavior my_target" can help you map user journeys, identify popular features, and gain insights into user demographics.

This information is valuable for market research, user experience optimization, and targeted marketing strategies.

Advanced profiling also extends to assessing the target's online reputation and brand perception.

Commands like "builtwith analyze online reputation my_target" can help you monitor mentions, reviews, and sentiment related to the target across various online platforms.

This analysis aids in reputation management and crisis response strategies.

Furthermore, advanced profiling encompasses the exploration of third-party integrations and APIs.

Commands like "builtwith analyze integrations my_target" can reveal the external services and platforms that interact with the target's website.

Understanding these integrations is crucial for assessing potential security risks and dependencies.

Advanced profiling is not limited to websites alone.

Commands like "builtwith analyze digital presence my_target" can be used to assess a target's overall online presence, including social media profiles, mobile applications, and other digital assets.

This holistic view provides a comprehensive understanding of the target's digital footprint.

Moreover, advanced profiling involves continuous monitoring and tracking of changes.

Commands like "builtwith analyze changes my_target" enable you to stay informed about alterations to the target's online properties, such as technology stack updates, content modifications, or structural changes.

This proactive approach helps you adapt your investigative strategies in real-time.

In summary, advanced profiling with BuiltWith elevates your OSINT capabilities by going beyond surface-level technology identification.

By analyzing architecture, behavior, content, data handling, user engagement, reputation, integrations, and digital presence, you gain a holistic view of your target's online footprint.

This in-depth understanding empowers you to make informed decisions, assess risks, and uncover hidden insights that can be invaluable for various investigative purposes.

Remember that advanced profiling is an ongoing process, and continuous monitoring ensures that you remain up-to-date with the evolving digital landscape of your target.

In-depth analysis of web technologies is a crucial aspect of open source intelligence, and it involves delving deep into the technical infrastructure of websites and online platforms.

To initiate this analysis, you can use commands like "analyze web technologies" followed by the target website's URL.

This process allows you to uncover the underlying technologies that power a website, such as content management systems (CMS), web servers, programming languages, and more.

Understanding the technology stack of a website provides valuable insights into its capabilities, security vulnerabilities, and potential points of attack or exploitation.

One of the primary components of web technology analysis is identifying the Content Management System (CMS) used by a website.

CMS platforms like WordPress, Joomla, or Drupal have specific characteristics and vulnerabilities that can be crucial for OSINT practitioners to recognize.

By using commands like "identify CMS," you can ascertain which CMS is in use and tailor your investigative approach accordingly.

In-depth analysis also involves examining the web server that hosts a website.

Commands like "analyze web server" allow you to determine the server's software and version, which can be essential for identifying potential security vulnerabilities and attack vectors.

Moreover, understanding the programming languages employed in a website's development can provide insights into its functionality and potential weaknesses.

Commands like "analyze programming languages" can reveal whether a website uses PHP, Python, Ruby, or other languages, helping you assess the coding quality and security aspects.

In-depth analysis extends to identifying the presence of specific web frameworks and libraries.

Commands like "detect web frameworks" enable you to pinpoint whether a website relies on frameworks like Angular, React, or Vue.js, which can influence its performance and security.

Moreover, analyzing the use of JavaScript libraries can unveil additional functionalities and potential entry points for investigations.

Advanced web technology analysis also involves assessing the website's SSL/TLS certificate.

Commands like "analyze SSL/TLS certificate" can reveal certificate details, including the issuer, expiration date, and any potential security issues, such as weak encryption algorithms or expired certificates.

Furthermore, in-depth analysis encompasses the examination of web security headers.

Commands like "inspect security headers" allow you to check if a website implements security headers like Content Security Policy (CSP), HTTP Strict Transport Security (HSTS), or X-Content-Type-Options, which can indicate its commitment to user security.

Understanding the use of web analytics tools is another facet of web technology analysis.

Commands like "check for web analytics" can uncover the presence of tools like Google Analytics, Matomo, or Mixpanel, which provide insights into user behavior and engagement.

Analyzing the website's use of advertising and tracking scripts is also crucial.

Commands like "scan for tracking scripts" can help identify the presence of third-party trackers, which can raise privacy concerns and inform you about data collection practices.

Furthermore, in-depth analysis of web technologies includes examining the website's database management system (DBMS).

Commands like "identify DBMS" can reveal whether the website uses MySQL, PostgreSQL, or other database systems, which can be essential for data retrieval and understanding the data storage architecture.

Moreover, assessing the use of APIs and external integrations is part of the comprehensive analysis.

Commands like "analyze APIs and integrations" can unveil connections to external services, which may pose security risks or provide avenues for further investigation.

In-depth analysis of web technologies also entails evaluating the website's performance optimization techniques.

Commands like "check performance optimizations" can help identify techniques like content delivery networks (CDNs), caching mechanisms, or image compression, which influence the site's speed and user experience.

Moreover, assessing the presence of security mechanisms such as firewalls, intrusion detection systems (IDS), or web application firewalls (WAF) is essential.

Commands like "examine security measures" can provide insights into the website's defense mechanisms against cyber threats and vulnerabilities.

Furthermore, in-depth analysis includes scrutinizing the website's use of cookies and tracking mechanisms.

Commands like "inspect cookies and trackers" can reveal the types of cookies used, their purpose, and whether the website complies with privacy regulations.

Lastly, understanding the website's use of third-party plugins and extensions is part of the comprehensive analysis.

Commands like "audit plugins and extensions" can identify any additional functionalities added to the website and potential security risks associated with them.

In summary, in-depth analysis of web technologies is a multifaceted process that involves examining various aspects of a website's technical infrastructure.

By using commands to identify CMS, web server, programming languages, frameworks, SSL/TLS certificates, security headers, web analytics tools, tracking scripts, DBMS, APIs, performance optimizations, security measures, cookies, and plugins/extensions, OSINT practitioners can gain a comprehensive understanding of a target's web technology stack.

This knowledge not only aids in assessing security vulnerabilities but also informs investigative strategies and helps uncover potential leads in OSINT endeavors.

Chapter 9: Specialized OSINT Approaches

Targeted OSINT strategies are essential for efficiently gathering specific information and insights from online sources.

Begin by defining clear objectives and goals for your OSINT investigation; commands such as "set objectives" can help you establish a precise focus.

Identify the specific information or data you need to collect, and use commands like "define data requirements" to articulate your needs.

Once your objectives are clear, it's essential to determine your target audience, as this influences the sources and methods you'll use. Use commands like "identify target audience" to refine your approach.

Understanding the target's online presence is crucial. Utilize commands like "analyze online presence" to evaluate websites, social media profiles, forums, and other digital channels.

Consider the potential digital footprints of your target and use commands like "trace digital footprints" to map out their online activities and interactions.

Effective OSINT often involves identifying key individuals or entities associated with your target. Commands like "identify key figures" can help pinpoint relevant personalities or organizations.

Furthermore, determining the target's digital habits and behaviors is essential. Use commands like "analyze digital behavior" to gain insights into their online routines and preferences.

Engaging with open source intelligence sources is a pivotal step. Commands like "access OSINT sources" can guide you to platforms, databases, and repositories of information relevant to your investigation.

Explore social media platforms, blogs, news websites, and public records using commands like "scrutinize social media" or "monitor news articles" to stay up-to-date with the latest developments related to your target.

Incorporate advanced search techniques by using commands like "utilize advanced search operators" to narrow down search results and discover hidden information.

Additionally, leverage tools like Metagoofil, theHarvester, Mitaka, and BuiltWith to extract data and metadata that may be relevant to your investigation.

To gather information from social media platforms, use commands like "extract social media data" to obtain posts, comments, and interactions that can provide valuable insights.

Consider the geolocation aspect of your investigation; use commands like "perform geolocation analysis" to identify the physical locations associated with your target.

Analyzing images and multimedia content can be crucial in OSINT. Use commands like "analyze multimedia content" to extract valuable data from photos, videos, and audio files.

Collaboration is key in targeted OSINT. Use commands like "coordinate with peers" to engage with fellow investigators and share findings and strategies.

Furthermore, maintain a detailed log of your activities and findings using commands like "create investigation log" to keep a record of your progress.

Privacy and ethics should always be considered. Commands like "adhere to ethical guidelines" remind you to respect privacy and comply with legal and ethical standards.

When dealing with sensitive or confidential information, use commands like "secure data handling" to ensure that the data you collect is handled securely and responsibly.

As you progress in your targeted OSINT investigation, continuously reassess your objectives and data requirements. Commands like "review objectives" help you adapt to changing circumstances.

Consider the potential risks and threats associated with your investigation, and use commands like "evaluate risks" to mitigate potential dangers.

Maintain good communication with your team and supervisors by using commands like "report progress" to provide updates on your investigation's status.

Furthermore, consider the potential legal and ethical implications of your actions, especially when dealing with sensitive or private information.

If necessary, use commands like "seek legal advice" to ensure that your OSINT activities are within legal boundaries.

Ensure that your findings are accurate and reliable by using commands like "verify information" to cross-reference data from multiple sources.

Consider the impact of your OSINT findings and how they may be used; commands like "assess implications" help you understand the potential consequences.

Lastly, remember that targeted OSINT is an iterative process. Use commands like "continuously improve strategies" to refine your approach based on your experiences and outcomes.

In summary, targeted OSINT strategies involve defining clear objectives, identifying relevant sources, utilizing advanced search techniques and tools, maintaining ethical practices, and continuously improving your investigative approach. By following these commands and principles, OSINT practitioners can effectively gather specific information and insights to support their objectives and goals.

OSINT, or Open Source Intelligence, has proven to be a

valuable asset across a wide range of industries and applications.

Its core principle of collecting and analyzing publicly available information to gain insights and make informed decisions can be adapted to various niche fields.

One such niche field where OSINT plays a crucial role is competitive intelligence, where businesses use open-source data to monitor their competitors' activities and strategies.

Commands like "analyze competitor data" allow organizations to keep tabs on their rivals, helping them stay ahead in the market.

In the world of law enforcement and security, OSINT is indispensable for tracking criminal activities and potential threats.

Law enforcement agencies can use commands like "investigate online threats" to monitor online forums and social media for signs of criminal intent.

In the realm of cybersecurity, OSINT is a vital tool for identifying vulnerabilities and potential risks to a company's digital infrastructure.

Commands such as "scan for cybersecurity threats" enable cybersecurity experts to stay vigilant against emerging threats.

The healthcare industry can benefit from OSINT by monitoring public health data and tracking disease outbreaks.

With commands like "analyze health data," health professionals can identify trends and take preventive measures.

In academia and research, OSINT aids in data collection and information gathering for various scholarly studies.

Commands like "gather research data" facilitate the collection of publicly available data for academic research.

In journalism and media, OSINT is used to verify information and fact-check stories.

Commands like "verify news sources" help journalists ensure the accuracy of their reporting.

Environmental organizations can employ OSINT to monitor and assess the impact of human activities on ecosystems.

Commands like "track environmental changes" enable environmentalists to gather data on deforestation, pollution, and climate change.

The legal field also relies on OSINT for tasks such as background checks and litigation support.

Commands like "conduct background checks" assist legal professionals in gathering relevant information about individuals and entities involved in legal cases.

In the world of politics, OSINT plays a significant role in monitoring public sentiment and assessing the impact of policies and campaigns.

Commands like "analyze political trends" help political analysts gain insights into the shifting political landscape.

Nonprofit organizations can leverage OSINT to gather data on potential donors and funding opportunities.

Commands like "research potential donors" enable nonprofits to identify potential sources of financial support.

Real estate professionals can use OSINT to gather data on property values, market trends, and potential investment opportunities.

Commands like "analyze real estate data" aid in property research and market analysis.

In the field of sports, OSINT can be used to monitor athlete performance and track sports-related trends.

Commands like "track athlete statistics" help sports analysts stay informed about players' achievements and team dynamics.

The entertainment industry can benefit from OSINT by analyzing audience sentiment and media trends.

Commands like "assess media reception" assist in understanding how the public perceives movies, music, and other forms of entertainment.

In the world of education, OSINT can be used to gather information on educational institutions, curriculum development, and academic research.

Commands like "research educational institutions" help educators and administrators make informed decisions.

Even in niche fields like paranormal investigation, OSINT can be applied to collect data on reported supernatural phenomena.

Commands like "investigate paranormal claims" can help paranormal researchers gather and analyze eyewitness accounts and evidence.

In summary, OSINT's adaptability and versatility make it a valuable asset in a wide range of niche fields and industries.

By utilizing the appropriate commands and methodologies tailored to their specific needs, professionals and organizations in these niches can harness the power of open-source intelligence to gain insights, make informed decisions, and achieve their goals.

Chapter 10: Real-world OSINT Applications and Case Studies

Practical OSINT use cases abound in today's information-driven world, offering invaluable insights and solutions across diverse domains.

"Explore OSINT Applications" and uncover how this powerful methodology is employed across various industries and professions.

In the realm of cybersecurity, OSINT proves indispensable by helping organizations proactively identify vulnerabilities and potential threats.

Commands like "Detect Cybersecurity Threats" empower cybersecurity experts to monitor online chatter and gather intelligence on potential attacks.

Law enforcement agencies have harnessed OSINT to investigate crimes and track down criminals.

With "Leverage OSINT for Criminal Investigations," law enforcement professionals can access a wealth of publicly available information to assist in solving cases.

Businesses are utilizing OSINT to gain a competitive edge by monitoring market trends, analyzing competitors, and assessing customer sentiment.

Commands such as "Conduct Market Research" enable companies to stay agile in the fast-paced business landscape.

Media organizations rely on OSINT to verify information, fact-check stories, and gather data for investigative journalism.

"Employ OSINT in Media Verification" to ensure accurate reporting and maintain journalistic integrity.

For the healthcare sector, OSINT aids in tracking disease outbreaks, monitoring public health data, and researching medical trends.

Commands like "Analyze Health Data" equip healthcare professionals with the insights needed to protect public health.

Environmentalists and conservationists use OSINT to assess the impact of human activities on ecosystems and advocate for sustainable practices.

With "Monitor Environmental Changes," activists can collect data on deforestation, pollution, and climate change.

In academia, OSINT assists researchers in data collection and information gathering for various scholarly studies.

Commands such as "Gather Research Data" facilitate the acquisition of publicly available data for academic purposes.

OSINT also plays a vital role in the legal field, supporting tasks like background checks, due diligence, and litigation support.

Commands like "Conduct Due Diligence" aid legal professionals in making informed decisions and building strong cases.

Political analysts rely on OSINT to monitor public sentiment, assess the impact of policies, and analyze political trends.

"Analyze Political Trends" and stay ahead of the ever-evolving political landscape.

Nonprofit organizations employ OSINT to identify potential donors, research funding opportunities, and expand their impact.

Commands like "Research Donors" help nonprofits connect with individuals and entities willing to support their missions.

Real estate professionals leverage OSINT to gather data on property values, market trends, and investment opportunities.

With "Analyze Real Estate Data," professionals can make informed decisions in the dynamic real estate industry.

In sports, OSINT aids in tracking athlete performance, analyzing sports-related trends, and assessing team dynamics.

Commands such as "Track Athlete Statistics" equip sports analysts with valuable insights for strategic planning.

The entertainment industry uses OSINT to gauge audience sentiment, assess media reception, and adapt content strategies.

"Assess Media Reception" and tailor entertainment offerings to meet audience preferences.

Educational institutions benefit from OSINT by researching competitors, analyzing curriculum trends, and gathering data on academic research.

Commands like "Research Educational Trends" empower educators to provide quality education in a rapidly evolving landscape.

Even in niche fields like paranormal investigation, OSINT can be applied to collect and analyze evidence of supernatural phenomena.

Commands like "Investigate Paranormal Claims" aid researchers in documenting and understanding unexplained events.

In each of these practical OSINT use cases, the ability to access, analyze, and leverage publicly available information is key to success.

By embracing OSINT methodologies and employing the appropriate commands, professionals across diverse sectors can harness its potential to make informed decisions, mitigate risks, and achieve their objectives.

"Dive into OSINT Success Stories" to discover how this

dynamic methodology has transformed real-world scenarios across various domains.

In the realm of cybersecurity, OSINT has been instrumental in identifying vulnerabilities, tracking potential threats, and enhancing overall digital security.

Commands like "Uncover Cybersecurity Successes" allow organizations to fortify their defenses and safeguard sensitive information.

Law enforcement agencies have harnessed the power of OSINT to solve complex cases, locate fugitives, and dismantle criminal networks.

With the command "Achieve Success in Law Enforcement," law enforcement professionals can access crucial data and intelligence to facilitate investigations.

Businesses of all sizes have leveraged OSINT to gain a competitive edge by monitoring market trends, analyzing competitors, and understanding consumer sentiment.

Commands such as "Achieve Business Success" empower companies to make data-driven decisions and adapt to the ever-changing marketplace.

Media organizations have increasingly relied on OSINT to verify information, fact-check stories, and uncover hidden truths in investigative journalism.

"Realize Success in Media Verification" and uphold journalistic integrity in an era of information overload.

In the healthcare sector, OSINT has played a pivotal role in tracking disease outbreaks, monitoring public health data, and researching medical trends.

Commands like "Attain Success in Healthcare" equip healthcare professionals with the insights needed to protect public well-being.

Environmentalists and conservationists have embraced OSINT to assess the impact of human activities on ecosystems and advocate for sustainable practices.

With the command "Promote Environmental Success," activists can collect and analyze data to drive positive change.

In academia, researchers have tapped into OSINT to gather data, conduct surveys, and collect information for various scholarly studies.

Commands such as "Achieve Academic Success" facilitate the acquisition of publicly available data for research purposes.

Legal professionals have integrated OSINT into their practices, using it for background checks, due diligence, and litigation support.

Commands like "Excel in Legal Practice" aid lawyers in building strong cases and making informed decisions.

Political analysts have turned to OSINT to gauge public sentiment, assess policy impacts, and gain insights into political dynamics.

"Navigate Political Success" and stay ahead of the ever-evolving political landscape.

Nonprofit organizations have employed OSINT to identify potential donors, research funding opportunities, and expand their outreach.

Commands such as "Foster Nonprofit Success" help nonprofits connect with supporters who share their mission.

Real estate professionals have harnessed OSINT to gather data on property values, market trends, and investment opportunities.

With the command "Thrive in Real Estate," professionals can make informed decisions in a dynamic industry.

In the world of sports, OSINT has aided in tracking athlete performance, analyzing sports-related trends, and assessing team dynamics.

Commands like "Succeed in Sports Analysis" equip analysts with valuable insights for strategic planning.

The entertainment industry has employed OSINT to gauge audience sentiment, assess media reception, and tailor content strategies.

"Achieve Entertainment Success" and create content that resonates with your target audience.

Educational institutions have benefited from OSINT by researching competitors, analyzing curriculum trends, and gathering data on academic research.

Commands such as "Succeed in Education" empower educators to provide quality learning experiences in a rapidly evolving landscape.

Even in niche fields like paranormal investigation, OSINT has been applied to collect and analyze evidence of supernatural phenomena.

With commands like "Achieve Paranormal Success," researchers can document and understand unexplained events.

In these case studies demonstrating OSINT success, the ability to access, analyze, and leverage publicly available information has been a game-changer.

By embracing OSINT methodologies and utilizing the appropriate commands, professionals across diverse sectors have harnessed its potential to make informed decisions, mitigate risks, and achieve their objectives.

Conclusion

In this comprehensive book bundle titled "OSINT Hacker's Arsenal," we have embarked on a journey through the fascinating world of Open Source Intelligence (OSINT). Across four distinct volumes, we have unraveled the intricacies of OSINT, from its foundational principles to advanced techniques and expert strategies. Let us take a moment to reflect on the knowledge gained and the journey we've undertaken.

In "Book 1 - OSINT Hacker's Arsenal: Unveiling the Essentials," we laid the groundwork for OSINT exploration, introducing novices to fundamental concepts and tools. We discovered the power of Metagoofil, theHarvester, Mitaka, and BuiltWith, learning how to extract valuable information from the vast sea of publicly available data.

"Book 2 - Mastering OSINT: Advanced Techniques with Mitaka" elevated our OSINT capabilities to a whole new level. We delved into the world of automation, customization, and integration, exploring Mitaka's potential for streamlining OSINT tasks and conducting in-depth investigations. Through case studies and best practices, we honed our skills as proficient OSINT practitioners.

"Book 3 - Expert OSINT Strategies: Harnessing BuiltWith for Profound Insights" unveiled the extensive possibilities offered by BuiltWith. We uncovered hidden gems within technology stacks, honed our competitive analysis skills, and applied BuiltWith in corporate investigations. The book provided profound insights into how this tool can be leveraged to gain a competitive edge and make informed decisions.

Finally, "Book 4 - The Ultimate OSINT Handbook: From Novice to Pro with Comprehensive Toolkits" brought our OSINT journey full circle. We transformed from novices to professionals, armed with comprehensive toolkits and a deep understanding of OSINT ethics and legal considerations. Real-world case studies demonstrated the practical application of our newfound expertise.

As we conclude this OSINT adventure, it's essential to recognize the ever-evolving nature of the field. OSINT remains a dynamic discipline, and staying at the forefront of its developments is paramount. Whether you're a novice eager to embark on your OSINT journey or an expert seeking to expand your repertoire, this book bundle has provided a solid foundation and a wealth of advanced insights.

We hope you've found the knowledge and skills shared within these pages invaluable for your OSINT endeavors. Remember that responsible and ethical OSINT practices are not only essential but also a moral obligation. As you continue to explore the world of OSINT, may you do so with integrity, respect for privacy, and a commitment to making informed decisions that benefit both individuals and organizations.

Thank you for joining us on this OSINT exploration. We wish you success and fulfillment in your future OSINT endeavors, and may your curiosity and dedication continue to drive you toward new horizons in the ever-expanding OSINT landscape.